KEY WORD INDEX
By Tom Henry

This index is designed to find references in the Code easily. Having worked in the electrical field for over 50 years as an apprentice, journeyman, master, electrical inspector, instructor, and author, I realize at times how difficult it is to "find it in the Code."

The Code is laid out in Articles and Chapters starting with Article 90, the introduction. Chapter 1 Article 100 is definitions, Article 110 is requirements for electrical installations. Chapter 2 is wiring and protection with Article 200 use and identification of grounded conductors, Article 210 branch circuits, 215 feeders, 220 calculations and so on. Chapters 2, 3 and 4 are the "meat" of the Code for the electrician in his daily work. Chapters 5, 6, 7 and 8 are for special applications such as hazardous locations, elevators, pools, mobile homes, studios, high-voltage, signs, health care facilities, etc. Chapter 9 is a special chapter with tables and examples.

The first part of the Article is for under 600 volts, the latter part of the Article is for over 600 volts. All the rules are not in the Electrical Code. Example: What is the minimum height of a ceiling paddle fan in a residence? You would find that information in the Mechanical Code.

110.3b in the Code is very important as it states, "all electrical equipment shall be installed as listed." Which means the directions of installation that come with the equipment must be followed.

•**Please Note** - In the **2011 National Electrical Code** ® the wording **FPN** has been replaced with the wording **Informational Note** indicated as *I.N.* in this edition of the Key Word Index.

Copyright © 2010 by Tom Henry. All rights reserved. No part of this publication may be reproduced in any form or by any means: electronic, mechanical, photo-copying, audio or video recording, scanning, or otherwise without prior written permission of the copyright holder.

While every precaution has been taken in the preparation of this book, the author and publisher assumes no responsibility for errors or omissions. Neither is any liability assumed from the use of the information contained herein.

National Electrical Code ® and NEC ® are Registered Trademarks of the National Fire Protection Association, Inc., Quincy, MA

2nd Printing ISBN 978-0-9801787-3-9

-A-

Term	Reference
A/C rated-load current	440.2 p.340
Abandoned outlets	390.8 p.239
Above floor level, garages	511.3C1(A) p.420
Above ground storage tanks	T.515.3 p.430
Aboveground conductors, install.	300.37 p.145
Abrasion	344.46 p.205
Abrasives	110.12(B) p.35
Absorbent materials	300.6(D) p.140
Absorbing regenerated power	620.91(A) p.543
AC - DC in same enclosure	300.3(C1) p.136
AC - DC in same enclosure	725.48(A) p.643
AC - DC, snap switch inductive	404.14(B2) p.269
AC - DC, tapped	210.10 p.51
AC adjustable motor, ampacity	430.6(C) p.311
AC cable, adequate path	320.108 p.187
AC cable, definition	320.2 p.186
AC cable, place of assembly	518.4(A) p.459
AC Cable, service	230.43 p.82
AC circuit less than 50v grounded	250.20(A) p.104
AC receptacle	210.63 p.58
AC resistance,	Table 9 p.722
AC snap switch	404.14(A) p.269
Accelerate their loads	440.54(B) p.346
Acceleration, motor	430.32(C) p.320
Access to elect. equipment	760.21 p.652
Access to elect. equipment	770.21 p.661
Access to elect. equipment	725.21 p.641
Access to elect. equipment	800.21 p.670
Access to elect. equipment	820.21 p.687
Access to manholes, dimensions	110.75(A) p.45
Access, electric equipment	110.26 p.37
Accessible, attics	320.23 p.186
Accessible, boxes	314.29 p.184
Accessible, electrode connection	250.68(A) p.115
Accessible, readily, disconnect A/C	440.14 p.343
Accessible, sign transformer	600.21(A) p.522
Accessible, switches 6' 7"	404.8(A) p.267
Accessible, to pedestrians	600.5(A) p.519
Accessory buildings, GFCI	210.8(A2) p.50
Accessory buildings, receptacles	210.52(G) p.58
Acetone	505.6(C) p.401
Acid or alkali type	700.12(A) p.624
Acrolein	500.6(A) ex.2 p.371
Adapter, polarized	406.10(B4) p.273
Adapters	240.54 p.96
Adapters, two-fers	520.69 p.467
Additional lighting outlets	110.26(D) p.39
Adequacy	90.1(B) p.22
Adequate access cable tray	392.18(F) p.240
Adequate bonding	250.116 *I.N.* p.122
Adequate compaction of fill	300.5(F) p.139
Adjacent light source	110.26(D) p.39
Adjacent to basin location	210.52(D) p.57
Adjustable speed drive	430.2 p.310
Adjustable speed drive, nonlinear	DEF 100 p.30
Adjustable speed drive system	430.122 p. 333
Adjustable trip circuit breaker	240.6(B) p.91
Adobe	334.10(B3) p.196
Aerial cable	382.12(2) p.233
AFCI, dwelling bedroom	210.12(B) p.52
AFCI, laundry room, No	210.12(B) p.52
Afford no protection	230.95(C) *I.N. #1* p.87
Aggregate	360.12 p.219
Agricultural buildings, wiring	547.5 p.478
Air cond. branch-circuit select.	440.6(A) ex.1 p.341
Air conditioner cord length	440.64 p.346
Air conditioner, disconnect location	440.14 p.343
Air conditioner, LCDI & AFCI	440.65 p.346
Air conditioners, plug connected	440.62(C) p.346
Air conditioners, room	440.62(C) p.346
Air conditioning equipment	440.1 p.340
Air ducts	250.104(B) *I.N.* p.119
Air handling spaces	300.22 p.144
Air handling spaces, type BLP	830.154(b) p.704
Air hoses	668.31 p.571
Air moving device	424.59 *I.N.* p.300
Air space	300.6(D) p.140
Air space, cabinets & cutout boxes	312.2 p.174
Air voids, romex	334.10(C2) p.196
Air, free circulation of	110.13(B) p.36
Air-break isolating switch	230.204(A) p.87
Aircraft fuel tanks	513.3(C) p.422
Aircraft hangar, underground wiring	513.8 p.423
Aircraft hangars, pit	513.3(A) p.422
Aircraft hangars, stock rooms	513.3(D) p.423
Aircraft hangars, ventilated	513.3(D) p.423
Airfield lighting cable	310.10(F) ex. 2 p.148
Airport runways	T.300.50 p.146
Airport runways, cable	T.300.5 p.138
Airspace for nometallic boxes	300.6(D) p.140
Alarm threshold value	517.160(B1) ex. p.458
Alarm threshold value	517.160(B2) ex. p.458
Alarm, burglar	800.2 p.669
Alarm, fire systems	760.1 p.651
Alerting system, alarm	517.32(C) p.447
Alkali-type battery cells	480.6(B) p.360
Alternate source for emerg. systems	700.26 p.627
Alternate source power, hospital	517.44(B) p.452
Aluminum bars, ampacity	366.23(A) p.223
Aluminum cond., wire bending space	T.312.6(B) p.176
Aluminum conductors CO/ALR	406.2(C) p. 270

Entry	Reference
Aluminum conductors size	310.106(B) p.171
Aluminum fittings & enclosures	358.12 ex. p.218
Aluminum grounding conductor	250.64(A) p.113
Aluminum inhibitor required	110.14 p.36
Aluminum neutral underground	230.30 ex.4 p.81
Aluminum not magnetic mat.	300.20(B) *I.N.* p.144
Aluminum siding, grounding	250.116 *I.N.* p.122
Amateur trans. station, ground	810.58(C) p.685
Amateur transmitting station	T.810.52 p.685
Ambient temp. exceeds 86°F	T.310.15(B)(16) p.154
Ambient temperature	310.10(1) p.149
Ambient Temperature	310.15 *I.N. #1* p. 149
American Wire Gage (AWG)	110.6 p.35
Ammeter conductors	300.3(C2c) p.136
Ammeter, anesthetizing	517.160(B3) *I.N.* p.458
Ammonia	500.6(A) 4 p.371
Ampacities, voltage drop	310.15 *I.N. #1* p. 149
Ampacity,	Annex B p.730
Ampacity,	DEF 100 p.26
Ampacity, 15 minute motor	T.610.14(A) p.529
Ampacity, adjustment factors	310.15(B3) p.150
Ampacity, aluminum	T.310.15(B)(16) p.154
Ampacity, aluminum bars	366.23(A) p.223
Ampacity, bare cond. & insulated	310.15(B4) p.152
Ampacity, bare conductor	310.15(B4) p.152
Ampacity, bare copper bars	366.23(A) p.223
Ampacity, bus bar	366.23(A) p.223
Ampacity, cables type W & G	T.400.5(A2) p.259
Ampacity, capacitor conductors	460.8(A) p.357
Ampacity, Class 1 conductors	725.49(A) p.644
Ampacity, conduit in free air	T. B.310.15(B2)(1) p.731
Ampacity, covered conductor	T. 310.21 p.157
Ampacity, extra-hard usage cords	T.520.44 p.463
Ampacity, feeder minimum	215.2(A) p.59
Ampacity, ferromagnetic envelope	426.40 p.306
Ampacity, fixture wires	402.5 p.266
Ampacity, flex. cords & cables	T.400.5(A1) p.258
Ampacity, free air	T.310.15(B)(17) p.155
Ampacity, generators	445.13 p.347
Ampacity, hoists & cranes	T.610.14(A) p.529
Ampacity, knob and tube wiring	T.310.15(B)(17) p.155
Ampacity, lowest value	310.15(A2) p.149
Ampacity, monorail hoist	T.610.14(A) p.529
Ampacity, motor feeder cond.	430.24 p.318
Ampacity, motor resistors	T.430.23(C) p.317
Ampacity, neutral conductor solar	705.95 p.635
Ampacity, NM-NMB cable	334.80 p.198
Ampacity, phase converter	455.6 p.355
Ampacity, power resistors	T.430.29 p.319
Ampacity, resistance welders	630.31 p.553
Ampacity, romex 60°C	334.80 p.198
Ampacity, selection	310.15(A2) p.149
Ampacity, solar neutral	705.95 p.635
Ampacity, solar system	690.8 p.597
Ampacity, stage lights	520.42 p.462
Ampacity, temperature rating	110.14(C) p.36
Ampacity, transformer tie	450.6(A2) p.351
Ampacity, tray cable	336.80 p.199
Ampacity, UF cable 60°C	340.80 p.201
Ampacity, welders	630.11 p.552
Ampacity, X-Ray equip.	517.73(B) *I.N.* p.456
Ampacity, X-ray momentary	660.6(B) p.566
Ampacity. armored cable	320.80 p.187
Ampere rating, circuit breakers	240.83(A) p.97
Ampere, excess of 2000	225.30(C) p.74
Ampere, fraction .5 and larger	p.804
Amplification	Art. 640 p.554
Amplifier output circuits	640.9(C) p.557
An appliance, infrared lamps	422.14 p.292
Anchoring, FCC cable	324.30 p.189
Anesthetics, flammable Class I	517.60(A2) p.452
Anesthetizing location remote cont.	517.63(D) p.454
Anesthetizing location, definition	517.2 p.440
Anesthetizing location, recept.	517.61(A5) p.453
Anesthetizing locations, lt. fixtures	517.63(C1) p.454
Anesthetizing, ammeter	517.160(B3) *I.N.* p.458
Angle pull, boxes	314.28(A2) p.183
Animal behavior or prod.	547.10(A) p.480
Animal confinement areas	547.10(A) p.480
Animal excrement, corrosive	547.1(B) p.478
Animated props	522.2 *I.N.* p.468
Annex B	p.730
Anodizing, electroplating	669.1 p.571
Antenna box barrier	810.18(C) p.683
Antenna conductors, clearance	820.44(4) p.687
Antenna grd. conductor #14	820.100(A3) p.689
Antenna systems, bonding jumper	810.100(D) p.690
Antenna systems, material	810.11 ex. p.682
Antenna, receiving station grd.	810.21(H) p.684
Antennas, indoor lead-ins	810.18(B) p.683
Antennas, radio-TV	225.19(B) p.73
Antennas, voltage to ground	810.16(B) p.683
Appliance garages	210.52(C5) p.57
Appliance, cord-plug disconnect	422.33(A) p.293
Appliance, fixed definition	550.2 p.481
Appliance, nonmotor overcur.	422.11(E) p.291
Appliance, outlet	210.50(C) p.55
Appliance, portable definition	550.2 p.481
Appliance, stationary definition	550.2 p.481
Appliances	Art. 422 p.290
Appliances in transit	551.60 p.500
Appliances, battery powered	517.64(E) p.455
Appliances, continuous load	422.10(A) p. 291
Appliances, cord polarity	422.40 p.294

Appliances, disconnect	422.31(A) p.293
Appliances, fastened in place 50%	210.23(A) p.54
Appliances, flatirons-smoothing	422.46 p.294
Appliances, live parts exposed	422.4 p.290
Appliances, nameplate marking	422.60(A) p. 295
Appliances, no nameplate O.C.P.	422.11(E) p.291
Appliances, overcurrent protection	422.11(A) p.291
Appliances, resistance-heating	422.11(F) p.291
Appliances, signal heat	422.42 p.294
Appliances, unit switches	422.34 p.294
Appliances, water heaters b.c.	422.13 p.292
Applicable derived system	250.146(D) p.127
Approved	110.2 p.34
Approved bushing fittings Class I	501.10(B)2 p.376
Approved power outlet	590.4(C) p.517
Approved stapling, heat cables	424.41(I) p.299
Appurtenance, architectural	110.26(F) p.39
Aquarium, shall be grounded	250.114(3)B p.122
Arc lamps, stage portable	520.61 p.466
Arc or thermal effect	500.2 p.367
Arc projectors, conductor size	540.13 p.477
Arc welders	630.11 p.552
Arc-fault cir. interrupter, dwelling	210.12(A) p.52
Arc-fault circuit interrupter,	DEF 210.12(A) p.52
Architectural appurtenance	110.26(F2) p.39
Arcing across discontinuities	501.125(B) *I.N. #2* p.384
Arcing effects, equipment	110.3(A6) p.34
Arcing equipment Class I	511.7(B1a) p.421
Arcing or suddenly moving parts	240.41 p.96
Arcing parts, electrical equipment	110.18 p.37
Area circular mils	Table 8 p.721
Area sq. inch, insulated conduct.	Table 5 p. 716
Area square inch, bare conduct.	Table 8 p.721
Area square inch, compact alum.	Table 5A p.720
Area square inch, conduit	Table 4 p.712
Armature lead, DC generator	445.12(E) p.347
Armature shunt resistor	430.29 p.318
Armored cable (BX) support	320.30 p.187
Armored cable, conductors	320.104 p.187
Armored cable, construction	320.100 p.187
Armored cable, exposed work	320.15 p. 186
Armored cable, floor joists	320.23(A) p.186
Armored cable, uses permitted	320.10 p.186
Armories, place of assembly	518.2 p.458
Arranged to drain, raceways	230.53 p.83
Arranged to drain. raceway on bldg.	225.22 p.73
Arrangement, phase	430.97(B) p.329
Array, solar system definition	690.2 p.594
Articles 511 through 517	510.1 p.419
Artificial illumination	700.2 *I.N.* p.622
As low as practicable, capacitor	460.8(B) p.357
Askarel-insulated, trans.	450.25 p.353
ASME rated & stamp. vessel	422.11(F3) p. 291
ASME rated & stamped vessel	424.22(B) p.297
Asphalt, heating cables	426.20(C)1 p.305
Assembly halls definition	518.2 p.458
Assembly, 100 or more persons	518.1 p.458
Assembly, concealed parts	545.2 p.477
Asymmetrical fault current	490.21(D4) p.362
Atomization charging	516.10(A) p.438
Atomizing heads, electrostat. equip.	516.10(A2) p.438
Attach. plug, first-make,last-break	250.124(A) p.124
Attachment plug	DEF 100 p.36
Attachment plug, motor disconnect	430.109(F) p.331
Attachment plug, X-Ray	517.72(C) p.455
Attachment plugs, cords	400.7(B) p.260
Attachment plugs, polarized	200.10(A) ex. p.47
Attachment point, service head	230.54(C) ex. p.83
Attachment to crossarms	800.44(A2) p.671
Attendant electrical trailing cable	90.2(B2) p.22
Attended self-service stations	514.11(B) p.429
Attic entrance, AC cable	320.23 p.186
Attic equipment	210.63 p.58
Attic, lighting outlet for storage	210.70(3) p.58
Attic, switch controlled light	210.70(C) p.59
Attic, switch controlled light	210.70(A3) p.58
Audible & visual indicators	517.19(E) ex. p.445
Audible & visual signal devices	700.6 p.623
Audio signal processing	Art. 640 p. 554
Audio signal processing,	DEF 640.2 p.554
Audio-program signals conductors	640.9(C) p.556
Auditoriums, place of assembly	518.2 p.458
Authority having jurisdiction	555.13(B3) p.514
Authority having jurisdiction	90.4 p.23
Authority having jurisition,	definition 100 p.26
Authority having jurisition,	definition Annex H p.821
Automatic lighting, prohibited	110.26(D) p.39
Automatic means, capacitors	460.28(B) p.358
Automatic sprinkler, transfor.	450.43(A) ex. p.354
Automatically deenergize	501.125(A)2 p.383
Automatically started, motors	430.35(B) p.321
Automatically starting, gen.	700.12(B1) p.625
Automatically transfering fuel	700.12(B3) p.625
Automotive diagnostic equip. GFCI	511.12 p.422
Automotive spray booths	516.4(D) ex.2 p.437
Automotive vehicles, not in Code	90.2(B1) p.22
Autotransformer, O.C.P.	450.4(A) ex. p.348
Autotransformer, circuit derived	210.9 p. 51
Autotransformer, cont. neutral	450.5 p.350
Autotransformer, dimmers	520.25(C) p.461
Autotransformer, fixtures	410.138 p.288
Autotransformer, Motor control circuit	430.82(B) p.328
Autotransformer, motor starter	430.82(B) p.328
Autotransformer, phase current	450.5 *I.N.* p.350

Autotransformers, rec. vehicle	551.20(E) p.492
Aux. gutters, sound equip.	640.7(A) p.556
Auxiliary equip. elect.-dis. lamp	410.104 p.286
Auxiliary gutters, ampacity	366.23 p.223
Auxiliary gutters, bus bar spacing	366.23 p.223
Auxiliary gutters, extend beyond	366.12 p.223
Auxiliary gutters, supplement wiring	366.10 p.222
Auxiliary gutters, support	366.30 p.223
Auxiliary nonelectric connections	668.31 p.571
Available current interrupting rating	110.9 p.35
Available fault current field marking	110.24(A) p.37
Avoid heating, by induction	300.20(A) p.144
AWG size, American Wire Gauge	310.120 p.173

-B-

Backfed c.b., omit the add. fastener	705.12(D6) p.632
Backfed c.b., suitable for such opert.	705.12(D5) p.632
Back-fed panelboard devices	408.36(D) p.276
Backfeed of possible current	690.9 *I.N.* p.598
Backfill, damage to raceways	300.5(F) p.139
Backstage, bare bulbs	520.47 p.463
Baffle plates next to heaters	424.59 *I.N.* p.300
Balancer sets, generators	445.12(D) p.347
Balancing branch circuits	210.11(B) p.51
Balconies, access working space	110.33(B) p.42
Balconies, clearance	230.9(A) p.79
Ballast compartment, THW	T.310.104(A) p.168
Ballast marking, fixture	410.74(A) p.285
Ballast supply. both paired fixtures	410.137(C) p.288
Ballast, autotransformers	410.138 p.288
Ballast, primary leads	300.3(C2b) p.136
Ballasts, amp rating	220.18(B) p.64
Ballasts, conductor within 3"	410.68 p.285
Ballasts, exposed	410.136(A) p.287
Ballasts, thermal protection	410.130(E1) p.287
Barbed wire	110.31 p.40
Bare bulbs, backstage	520.47 p.463
Bare conductor, ampacity	310.15(B4) p.152
Bare conductor, area sq.in.	Table 8 p.721
Bare conductor, concrete encased	250.50 ex. p.111
Bare conductors	310.15(B4) p.152
Bare copper concentric, type USE	338.100 p.201
Bare copper cond. underground	230.30 ex. p.81
Bare grounding conductor	310.15(B4) p.152
Bare lead sheath	110.36 p.43
Bare live parts, working clearance	T.110.26(A) p.38
Bare neutral alum. underground	230.30 ex. d p.81
Barns, wet & damp location	410.10(A) p. 281
Barriers, cabinets wiring space	312.11(D) p.177
Barriers, panelboard bus bars	408.3(A) p.274
Baseboard heaters, recepts.	424.9 *I.N.* p. 296
Basement garage, fluorescent lights	410.10(A) p.281
Basin, bathroom	210.52(D) p.57
Basin, receptacle adjacent	210.52(D) p.57
Bathroom basin recpts, within 36"	210.52(D) p.57
Bathroom, definition	DEF 100 p.26
Bathroom, no other outlets	210.11(C3) p.52
Bathroom, receptacle	210.52(D) p.57
Bathrooms O.C.P.	240.24(E) p.95
Bathrooms, GFCI	210.8(A1) p.50
Bathtub rim, light fixture	410.10(D) p.281
Batteries	Art. 480 p.359
Batteries, cell explosion	480.10(B) p.360
Batteries, cells in jars	480.6(B) p.360
Batteries, cells per tray	480.6(B) p.360
Batteries, emergency lts. 1 1/2hrs	700.12(A) p.624
Batteries, racks and trays	480.8(A) p.360
Batteries, stand-by power 87 1/2%	701.12(A) p.629
Batteries, vented cells flame arrest.	480.10(A) p.360
Batteries, volts per cell	480.2 *I.N.* p.359
Battery backup unit, BBU	840.1 *I.N.* p.707
Battery conductors, prime mover	480.4 p.359
Battery pack units emerg.power	700.12(F) p.625
Battery powered appliances	517.64(E) p.455
BBU (battery backup unit)	840.1 *I.N.* p. 707
Beating rain, receptacles	406.9(A) p.273
Below finished grade	300.5(D)1 p.139
Benchmark	626.22(B) p.549
Bending radius, armored cable	320.24 p.187
Bending radius, conductors	110.3(A3) p.34
Bending radius, conduit	T. 2 Chapt. 9 p.711
Bending radius, flex. metal	T. 2 Chapt. 9 p.711
Bending radius, gas cable	T.326.24 p.191
Bending radius, hi-voltage cable	300.34 p.145
Bending radius, lead-covered	300.34 p.145
Bending radius, metal clad cable	330.24 p.193
Bending radius, MI cable	332.24 p.195
Bending radius, nonshielded cables	300.34 p.145
Bending radius, romex	334.24 p.197
Bending radius, shielded cables	300.34 p.145
Bends, number in one run	344.26 p.204
Bends, rigid conduit	T. 2 Chapt. 9 p.711
Bent by hand ENT	362.2 p.220
Bent, parts	110.12(B) p.35
Berthing	555.1 p.513
Beverage dispensers cord connected	440.13 p.343
Binding screws or studs	110.14(A) p.36
Bipolar circuits warning label	690.7(E3) p.597
Bipolar photovoltaic array	DEF 690.2 p.594
Bi-plane examinations	517.73(A2) p.456
Black marking	322.120(C) p.188

Blanketing effect, dust	500.6(B3) *I.N. #2* p.372	Boxes, accessibility	314.29 p.184
Block,	DEF 800.2 p.669	Boxes, angle or U pulls	314.28(A2) p.183
Blocking diode, DEF	690.2 p.594	Boxes, barriers	314.28(D) p.183
Blocks, power distribution	314.28(E) p.183	Boxes, bushings	314.42 p.185
BLP cable	830.179(B1) p.705	Boxes, cable clamps	314.16(B2) p.178
BLU cable	830.179(B5) p.707	Boxes, cable entry/exit over 600v	314.71(B1) p.185
BLX cable	830.179(B4) p.707	Boxes, cast metal	314.40(B) p.184
BM cable	830.179(A2) p.705	Boxes, combustible walls	314.20 p.180
BMR cable	830.179(A1) p.705	Boxes, conductors racked up	314.28(B) p.183
BMU cable	830.179(A3) p.705	Boxes, corrosion-resistant	314.40(A) p.184
Boat hoists	210.8(C) p. 51	Boxes, covers suitable for condit.	314.28(C) p.183
Boat slip	T.555.12 note 1 p.514	Boxes, Danger High-voltage	314.72(E) p.186
Boat, condominiums	555.1 p.513	Boxes, domed covers	314.16(A) p.178
Boatyards & marinas	Art. 555 p.513	Boxes, emergency circuits	700.10(A) p.623
Body of water, pools	680.1 p.575	Boxes, enclosing flush devices	314.19 p.180
Boiler, stamped vessel	424.72(A) p.301	Boxes, extension rings	314.16(A) p.178
Boilers, electrode type	424.82 p.301	Boxes, fixture studs	314.16(B3) p.178
Boilers, elements subdivided	424.72(B) p.301	Boxes, floor listed for application	314.27(B) p.183
Boilers, resistance type	424.70 p.300	Boxes, hickeys	314.16(B3) p.178
Bolted connections, services	230.46 p.82	Boxes, hi-voltage marking	314.72(E) p.186
Bolts, screws, or rivets	314.23(D1) p.181	Boxes, in wall or ceiling	314.20 p.180
Bolts, screws, or rivets	410.36(B) p.282	Boxes, internal depth	314.24 p.182
Bonded, cablebus framework	370.3 p.227	Boxes, malleable iron	314.40(B) p.184
Bonding all piping	250.104(B) *I.N.* p.119	Boxes, marking	314.44 p.185
Bonding electrodes, comm.	800.100(D) p.674	Boxes, NM cable extend 1/4"	314.17(C) p.180
Bonding jumpers main & equip.	250.102(A) p.118	Boxes, nonmetallic	314.17(C) p.180
Bonding jumpers size	T.250.66 • 250.30(A3A) p.107	Boxes, nonmetallic	314.3 p.177
Bonding metal air ducts	250.104(B) *I.N.* p.119	Boxes, nonmetallic	314.43 p.185
Bonding to assure continuity	250.90 p.117	Boxes, not required	398.42 p.250
Bonding well casings	250.112(M) p.121	Boxes, number of wires	314.16(A1) p.178
Bonding, Class I, Div. 1 & 2	501.30(A) p.381	Boxes, organic coatings raintight	300.6(A) p.139
Bonding, structural steel	250.104(C) p.120	Boxes, over 100 cubic inch	314.40(C) p.184
Booted or nonbooted plug	555.19(A1) p.515	Boxes, over 6 feet	314.28(B) p.183
Border lights, ampacity	T.520.44 p.462	Boxes, over 600 volts angle pull	314.71(B) p.185
Border lights, stage	520.41 p.462	Boxes, over 600 volts straight pull	314.71(A) p.185
Bored holes in wood	300.4(A1) p.136	Boxes, paddle fans	314.27(D) p.183
Bottom shield, FCC cable	324.2 p.189	Boxes, pendant supports	314.23(H) p.181
Bowling lanes, 100 people	518.2(A) p.458	Boxes, permanent barriers	314.28(D) p.183
Bowling lanes, place of assembly	518.2 p.458	Boxes, plaster rings	314.16(A) p.178
Box fill, light fixture wires	314.16(B1)ex. p.178	Boxes, porcelain covers	314.41 p.185
Box, double volume	314.16(B4) p.178	Boxes, pull and junction	314.28(A) p.183
Box, lightweight luminaire	314.27ex. p.182	Boxes, round	314.2 p.177
Box, number of extensions	314.16(A) p.178	Boxes, shall have a cover	314.25 p.182
Box, number of extensions	314.22 p.180	Boxes, shallow 1/2" internal depth	314.24(A) p.182
Box, opposite wall	314.28(A2) p.183	Boxes, show windows	314.27(C) ex. p.183
Box, paddle fan	314.27(D) p. 183	Boxes, straight pulls	314.28(A1) p.183
Box, plugging	530.2 p.472	Boxes, straight pulls over 600v	314.71(A) p.185
Box, scatter	530.2 p.472	Boxes, support light fixture	314.27(A) p.182
Box, splice temporary wiring	590.4(G) p.517	Boxes, support metal braces	314.23(B2) p.180
Boxes	Art. 314 p.177	Boxes, support of ceiling fans	314.27(D) p.183
Boxes, 100 cubic inch	314.40(B) p.184	Boxes, thickness of metal	314.40(B) p.184
Boxes, 15/16" in depth	314.24(B5) p.182	Boxes, threaded hub	314.23(E) p.181

Boxes, unused openings	110.12(A) p.35	Branch circuits, data processing	645.5 p.561
Boxes, volume per wire	T. 314.16(B) p. 178	Branch circuits, min. ampacity	210.19(A1) p.52
Boxes, wet location	314.15(A) p.177	Branch circuits, originate	590.4(C) p.517
Boxes, where required	300.15(A) p.142	Branch circuits, over 50 amp	210.23(D) p.55
Boxes, without devices	314.23(E) p.181	Branch circuits, signs	600.5(A) p.519
Boxes, wood brace support	314.23(B2) p.180	Branch circuits, small appl. 20a	210.52(B1) p.56
Boxes, yoke or strap	314.16(B4) p.178	Branch circuits, small appliance	210.11(C1) p.52
Boxless device	300.15(E) p.142	Branch-circuit selection	440.4(C) p.341
Boxless device NM and NMC	334.30(C) p.198	Brazed or welded	410.30(B2) p.282
Braces or guys, service mast	230.28 p.80	Breaker, height from floor	240.24(A) p.95
Bracket wiring, scenery	520.63(A) p.466	Breaker, highest location	240.24(A) p.95
Brackets open wiring outdoors	225.12 p.72	Breakers, as switches	404.11 p.268
Brackets or cleats TC cable	336.12 p.199	Breakers, as switches SWD	240.83(D) p.97
Braid covered conductors, open runs	300.39 p.145	Breakers, maximum number	408.54 p.277
Braid covered insulated conductors	300.39 p.145	Breakers, next higher size	240.4(B) p.90
Braided outer covering	110.36 p.43	Breakers, standard sizes	240.6 p.91
Braided-covered conductors	300.39 p.145	Breakfast room receptacles	210.52(B1) p.56
Branch circuit, air conditioner	440.1 p.340	Breakout assembly, DEF	520.2 p.460
Branch circuit, appliances	422.10 p.290	Bridge expansion joints	424.44(C) p.300
Branch circuit, balanced	210.11(B) p.51	Bridge frame, grounding	610.61 p.532
Branch circuit, bathroom	210.52(D) p.57	Bridge wire conductors	610.21(D) p.530
Branch circuit, busway	368.12 p.225	Brittle	378.10(3) *I.N.* p.231
Branch circuit, calculation	220.10 p.61	Brittle, nonmetallic conduits	352.10 *I.N.* p.208
Branch circuit, classification	210.3 p.48	Broadband communications systems	Art. 840 p.707
Branch circuit, color coding	210.5(C) p.49	Broadband, premises-powered	Art. 840 p.707
Branch circuit, combo loads	210.20(A) p.53	Broken, parts	110.12(B) p.35
Branch circuit, continuous	210.20(A) p.53	Building component definition	545.2 p.477
Branch circuit, cook equip. demand	Note 4 p.66	Building disconnecting means	225.39(B) p.75
Branch circuit, cord-plug 80%	210.23(A) p.54	Building exceeds 3 stories 50'	225.19(E) p.73
Branch circuit, extensions	210.12(B) p.52	Building surface wiring	225.10 p.72
Branch circuit, fixed appl. 50%	210.23(A) p.54	Building system definition	545.2 p.477
Branch circuit, heat	424.3 p.296	Buildings, accessory	210.52(G) p.58
Branch circuit, individual	210.3 p.48	Buildings, unfinished accessory	210.8(A2) p.50
Branch circuit, maximum load	220.18 p.63	Bulk storage plants	Art. 515 p.429
Branch circuit, maximum voltage	210.6 p.49	Bull-switches, motion pictures	530.15(D) p.473
Branch circuit, motors	430.22(A) p.316	Bundled conductors 3 or more	310.15(B3)(5) p.152
Branch circuit, multioutlet	210.3 p.48	Burglar alarm systems	725.1 p.641
Branch circuit, multiwire	210.4 p.48	Burial depths Class 1 Div.I	514.8 ex.2 p.428
Branch circuit, neutral conductor	200.4 p.46	Burial depths minimum cover	T.300.5 p.138
Branch circuit, number req.	Example 1a p.804	Buried cable over 600v depth	T.300.50 p.146
Branch circuit, O.C.P. motors	T.430.52 p.323	Burrs and fins, fixtures	410.62(A) p.284
Branch circuit, patient bed	517.19(A) p.444	Bus bar ampacity	366.23 p.223
Branch circuit, permissible loads	210.23 p.54	Bus bar spacing motors	T.430.97 p.330
Branch circuit, range neutral	210.19(A3) ex.2 p.53	Busbar arrangements	408.3(E) p.274
Branch circuit, ranges	210.19(A3) p.53	Busbar, clearance insulated	T.408.5 p.275
Branch circuit, rating	210.3 p.48	Busbar, clearance noninsulated	T.408.5 p.275
Branch circuit, stage lights	520.41 p.462	Busbars, insulated spacing	T.408.5 p.275
Branch circuit, standard classification	210.3 p.48	Busbars, motor control center	430.97 p.329
Branch circuit, water heater	422.13 p.292	Busbars, noninsulated spacing	T.408.5 p. 275
Branch circuits required	210.11 p.51	Bushed hole, raceway or cable	300.16(A) p.142
Branch circuits, 30 amp	210.23(B) p.54	Bushed openings	230.54(E) p.84
Branch circuits, 40-50 amp	210.23(C) p.55	Bushing in lieu of box or terminal	300.16(B) p.142

Bushing, #4 and larger conductor	300.4(G) p.137
Bushing, abrasion	352.46 p.210
Bushing, cable to conduit	300.5(H) p.139
Bushing, in lieu of box	300.16(B) p.142
Busway, barriers & seals	368.234(A) p.226
Busway, branch circuit	368.17(D) p.225
Busway, disconnecting links	368.239 p.226
Busway, overcurrent protection	368.17 p.225
Busway, plug-in cord	368.56(B2) p.226
Busway, reduction in size	368.17(B) p.225
Busway, temperature rise	368.214 p.226
Busways, inside & outside	368.234(A,B) p.226
Busways, support	368.30 p.225
Busways, unbroken lengths	368.10(C) p.224
Butadiene	500.6(A2) ex.1 p.371
Bypass isolation switch	DEF 100 p.32
Bypass isolation switches	700.5(B) p.623
Bypassing surge current	DEF 100 p.32

-C-

Cab. & cutout boxes, meter loops	312.11(C) p.177
Cabinets & cutout boxes, depth	312.11(B) p.177
Cabinets, air space 251 volts	312.11(A3) p.177
Cabinets, damp-wet location	312.2 p.174
Cabinets, plugs or plates	110.12(A) p.35
Cabinets, side-wiring spaces	312.11(D) p.177
Cabinets, wire bending space	T.312.6(A) p.175
Cabinets-cutout box, live parts	312.11(A3) p.177
Cabinets-cutout box, weatherproof	312.11(A) p.176
Cabinets-cutout boxes, doors	312.11(A2) p.177
Cabinets-cutout boxes, strength	312.10(B) p.176
Cabinets-cutout boxes, thickness	312.10(B) p.176
Cabinets-cutout boxes, wet location	312.2 p.174
Cable, airfield lighting	310.10(F) ex. 2 p.148
Cable armors	300.12 p.141
Cable assemblies	250.86 ex.2 p.117
Cable assemblies	300.12 ex.1 p.141
Cable clamps, deduction of wire	314.16(B2) p.178
Cable limiters	230.82 p.85
Cable management	626.23 p.549
Cable markings, CATV	T.820.179 p.693
Cable markings, Class I,II,III	T.725.154(G) p.648
Cable markings, communication	T.800.179 p.680
Cable markings, fire cable	T.760.176(G) p.659
Cable markings, fire cable	T.760.179(I) p.660
Cable markings, optical fiber	T.770.179 p.666
Cable protection, motion picture	530.18(C) p.474
Cable sheathing, protect from corr.	300.6 p.139
Cable sheaths	300.12 p.141
Cable substitutions Class I,II,III	T.725.154(G) p.648
Cable substitutions, CATV	T.820.154(B) p.693
Cable substitutions, comm.	T.800.179 p.680
Cable substitutions, fire	T.760.154(D) p.658
Cable substitutions, optical	T.770.154(B) p.666
Cable tray support service conductors	230.44 p.82
Cable tray system definition	392.2 p.239
Cable tray, metal equipment grding	392.60(B) p.245
Cable tray, nonmetallic	392.100(F) p.246
Cable tray, single conductor #1/0	392.10(B1a) p.240
Cable trays, cable Class I,II,III	725.3(E) p.641
Cable trays, cable splices	392.56 p.244
Cable trays, covered 6 feet	392.80(A1b) p.245
Cable trays, direction & elevation	392.100(E) p.246
Cable trays, edges, burrs, project.	392.100 p.246
Cable trays, elect. continuity	392.18(A) p.240
Cable trays, excessive movement	392.20(C) p.241
Cable trays, hoistways	392.12 p.240
Cable trays, maintained space	392.80(B2B) p.246
Cable trays, side rails	392.100(D) p.246
Cable trays, strength & rigidity	392.100(A) p.246
Cable trays, support instructions	392.30 p.243
Cable, deflecting junction box	300.19(C3) p.144
Cable, elevator type & uses	T.400.4 p.251
Cable, irrigation	675.4 p.573
Cable, plenum	T.725.154(G) p.648
Cable, portable power	T.400.4 p.257
Cable, power-limited tray	T.725.154(G) p.648
Cable, range and dryer	T.400.4 p.256
Cable, ribbon	522.21(B) p.469
Cable, riser Class I,II,III	T.725.154(G) p.648
Cable, support of other cables	300.11(C) p.141
Cable, trailing	90.2(B2) p.22
Cable, travel elevator note 5	T.400.4 p.257
Cablebus framework, bonded	370.3 p.227
Cablebus, conductor supports	370.4(D) p.227
Cablebus, exposed work	370.3 p.227
Cablebus, through dry floors	370.6(C) p.227
Cabled outlet, communications	800.156 p.678
Cables, ampacity	T.400.5(A)(1) p.258
Cables, coaxial fire signaling	760.179(H) p.659
Cables, hazardous location	725.3(D) p.641
Cables, heating	424.34 p.298
Cables, laid in notches of studs	300.4(A2) p.136
Cables, nonheating leads	424.34 p.298
Cables, portable over 600v	400.31 p.261
Cables, stage O.C.P. 400%	530.18(A) p.474
Cables, traveling elevator	620.12(A1) p.535
Cables, types W & G ampacity	T.400.5(A2) p.259
Cables, wet locations	310.10(C) p.148
Cadmium approved corrosion rest.	300.6(A) p.139
Calculated number of cond. .8	Table 1 note 7 p.711

Entry	Reference
Calculations, examples	p.804-815
Calculations, mobile homes	550.12 p.484
Calculations, rec. veh. park	T.551.73(A) p.501
Camping trailer definition	551.2 p.490
Can be started, motors	430.7(B1) p.313
Candelabra-base lampholders	410.54(B) p.283
Canned pumps	501.17 p.380
Canneries, indoor wet location	300.6(D) p.140
Canopies, space fixtures	410.20 p.282
Canopy	314.25 p.182
Capacitors	Art. 460 p.357
Capacitors induction heat	665.24 p.568
Capacitors, ampacity conductors	460.8(A) p.357
Capacitors, case not grounded	250.110 ex.1 p.121
Capacitors, connection to term.	460.28(B) p.358
Capacitors, discharge circuit	460.28(B) p.358
Capacitors, disconnection	460.28(B) p.358
Capacitors, dust Class II Div.1	502.100(A1) p.388
Capacitors, group-oper. switches	460.24(A) p.358
Capacitors, guarding accident contact	460.2(B) p.357
Capacitors, induction heating	665.24 p.568
Capacitors, O.C.P.	460.25 p.358
Capacitors, overcurrent	460.8(B) p.357
Capacitors, phase converter	455.23 p.357
Capacitors, Residual volt. reduction	460.28(A) p.358
Capacitors, surge-protective	502.35 p.388
Capacitors, vaults	460.2(A) p.357
Capped elbows	314.16(C3) p.179
Car house, railway conductors	110.19 ex. p.37
Car houses	110.19 ex. p.37
Car light, disconnect elevators	620.53 p.541
Car lights, elevator	620.22(A) p.538
Carbon black	500.6(B2) p.372
Carbon dioxide, transformers	450.43 ex. p.354
Carpet squares, FCC cable	324.1 p.189
Carries the electric signal	430.2 p.311
Cartridge fuses	240.60 p.97
Catalog number, heating element	426.25 p.306
Catenary angle, shore power cord	555.19(A2) p.515
Catheter	517.11 *I.N.* p.443
CATV cable	820.179(C) p.695
CATV systems	820.1 p.686
CATV, cable burial depth "NONE" found in Chapter 8	
CATV, cable conduit fill	820.110(B) p.690
CATV, coaxial grounding cond.	820.100(D) p.690
CATV, grounding metal sheath	800.93 p.673
CATV, lightning conductors	820.44(E3) p.688
CATVP cable	820.179(A) p.693
CATVR cable	820.179(B) p.693
CATVX cable	820.179(D) p.695
Cause discomfort	702.2 *I.N.* p.630
Caustic alkalis, MC cable	330.12(2b) p.193
Caution ... volts, tubing marking	410.146 p. 289
Caution signs, de-icing equipment	426.13 p.305
Ceiling fan, height over pool	680.22(B1) p. 579
Ceiling fan, height over spa	680.43(B1b) p. 587
Ceiling fans, support	422.18 p.293
Ceiling framing member	410.36(B) p.282
Ceiling support wires	300.11(A) p.141
Ceiling surface, heating cables	424.41(E) p.299
Cell explosion, batteries	480.10(B) p.360
Cell line conductors	668.12 p.570
Cell line definition	668.2 p.569
Cell line working zone	668.10 p.569
Cells in jars, batteries	480.6(C) p.360
Cellular concrete floor race., cond.	372.10 p.228
Cellular concrete floor raceway	372.1 p.228
Cellular metal floor raceway	374.1 p.229
Cellulose fiberboard	410.136(B) p.288
Cellulose nitrate film vaults	530.51 p.475
Celsius of the gas or vapor	501.125(B) p.384
Center conductor	T.400.4 note 7 p.257
Centerline, hallway receptacle	210.52(H) p.58
Central alarm system, branch circuit	210.25(B) p.55
Centralized distribution, sound	640.1 p.554
Ceramic floor, FCC cable	324.10(C) p.189
Chafing of cables	555.13(B4)(5) p.514
Chain supported light fixtures	410.14 p.281
Chains, fixture	410.56(E) p.284
Chair lifts	620.1 p.532
Charcoal	500.6(B2) p.372
Charge controller, DEF	690.2 p.594
Charging electrodes, spray appl.	516.10(A) p.438
Chemical de-icers	300.6(D) *I.N.* p.140
Chimes	620.2 p.533
Chimney or flue, transformers	450.25 p.353
Chimneys	225.19(B) p.73
Christmas tree lighting	410.54(B) p.283
Church chapels, place of assembly	518.2 p.458
Cinder fill, IMC	342.10(C) p.202
Cinder fill, rigid metal conduit	344.10(C) p.204
Circuit breaker marked 1ø - 3ø	240.85 p.97
Circuit breaker, voltage rating	240.85 p.97
Circuit breaker, 4-pole	445.12(E) p.347
Circuit breaker, adjustments	240.82 p.97
Circuit breaker, double-coil	445.12(E) p.347
Circuit breaker, enclosure	312.8 p.175
Circuit breaker, highest location	404.8(A) p.267
Circuit Breakers, ampere rating	240.83(A) p.97
Circuit breakers, as switches	404.11 p.268
Circuit breakers, as switches SWD	240.83(D) p.97
Circuit breakers, handles/levers	240.41(B) p.96
Circuit breakers, indicating	240.81 p.97
Circuit breakers, interrupt. rating	240.83(C) p.97

Circuit breakers, max. number	408.54 p.277
Circuit breakers, oil	490.21(D) p.362
Circuit breakers, standard sizes	240.6(A) p.91
Circuit breakers, trip free	240.80 p.97
Circuit directory, panelboard	408.4 p.275
Circuit interrupting devices over 600v	490.21 p.361
Circuit transfer, port. switchboard	520.50(B) p.464
Circuits derived from transformers	215.11 p.60
Circuits less than 50 volts	Art. 720 p.640
Circuits less than 50v, conductors	720.4 p.640
Circuits less than 50v, lampholders	720.5 p.640
Circular raceways	310.15(B3)(c) p.152
Circular mil area	Table 8 p.721
Circular mil area, compensate VD	250.122(B) p.124
Class 2 & 3 cir., wiring meth.	725.127 p.645
Class 2 & 3 circuits	725.121 p.644
Class 2 & 3 conductor support	725.143 p.647
Class 2 or 3, hoistways	725.136(H) p.646
Class 20 or 30 overload relay	430.32(C) *I.N.* p.320
Class I cir grd electrode cond.	250.30(A5)ex.#3 p.108
Class I circuits power limited	725.41(A) p.642
Class I circuits, conductors	725.49 p.644
Class I control circuits raceway	725.48 p.643
Class I Div. 1 - 2 under. wiring	514.8 ex.2 p.428
Class I Division 2, receptacle	501.105(B6) p.382
Class I location sealing compound	501.15 p.377
Class I Zone 0 locations NPT	505.9(E) p.405
Class I Zone 1 locations NPT	505.9(E) p.405
Class I Zone 2 locations NPT	505.9(E) p.405
Class I, Class 2, & Class 3 circuits	Art. 725 p.641
Class I, Div. 1 & 2 bonding	501.30(A) p.381
Class I, Div. 1-2 seal thickness	501.15(A3) p.378
Class I, Div. 2 isolating switch	501.115(B2) p.383
Class I, Div. 2 overcurrent prot.	501.115(B) p.382
Class I, Div.1 motors & generators	501.125(A) p.383
Class I, Div.1 wiring methods	501.10(A) p.376
Class I, Div.1 location flr. - ceiling	517.60(A2) p.453
Class I, Div.1 pendant fixtures	501.130(A3) p.384
Class I, Div.1 seals adjacent to box	501.15(A1) p.378
Class I, Div.2 sealing fitting	501.15(B2) p.378
Class I, Div.2 wiring methods	501.10(B) p.376
Class I, Group C type receptacle	517.61(A5) p.453
Class II location combustible dust	500.5(C) p.370
Class II locations	Art. 502 p.386
Class II max. O.C.P.	725.127 p.645
Class II, Div. 1 flexible connect.	502.10(A2) p.386
Class II, Division 1 location	500.5(C1) p.370
Class III Div. 1, boxes and fittings	503.10(A1) p.391
Class III locations	Art. 503 p.391
Class III, Div.1 & 2 motors & gen.	503.125 p.393
Class III, Division 2 location	500.5(D2) p.371
Classroom, school cooking	T.220.55 Note 5 p.66
Clean air purging	501.125(B) *I.N.* #2 p.384
Clean surfaces, continuity	250.12 p.103
Cleaners	110.12(B) p.35
Cleaning & lub. compounds	110.11 *I.N.* #2 p.35
Clearance of bare live parts	366.100(E) p.224
Clearances, service drop	230.24(B) p.80
Clearances, signs	225.19(B) p.73
Clearances, working	T.110.26(A1) p.38
Clearly and durably identified 10'	344.120 p.205
Cleat-type lampholders	410.5 p.280
Cleat-type receptacles	410.5 p.280
Climatic temperature zone	T.626.11(B) p.549
Climbing space, poles outdoors	225.14(D) p.72
Climbing space, through cond.	800.44(A3) p.671
Clips identified for use	314.23(C) p.180
Clips identified for use	410.36(B) p.282
Clock motors	430.32(B4) *I.N.* p.320
Clock motors, can not damage	430.81(A) p.327
Clock, electric outlet	210.52(B2) ex.1 p.56
Closed construction definition	545.2 p.477
Closet, light fixture height	410.16 p.281
Clothes closets, fixtures	410.16 p.281
Clothes closets, overcurrent device	240.24(D) p.95
Clothes dryer, grounded cond.	250.140 ex. p.126
Clothes dryer, neutral 70%	220.61(B1) p.67
Clothes dryers, demand factor	T.220.54 p.65
Clothes dryers, feeder load	220.54 p.65
Clothes hanging rod	410.2 p.280
Clothes washer/dryer	Example 2(B) p.805
Clothes washers, rec. vehicle	551.2 *I.N.* p.490
CM cable, communications cable	800.179(D) p.681
CMA, circular mil area	Table 8 p.721
CMP cable	800.179(A) p.680
CMR cable	800.179(B) p.681
CMUC cable	800.179(F) p.681
CMX cable	800.179(E) p.681
CO/ALR receptacles	406.2(C) p.270
CO/ALR snap switches	404.14(C) p.269
Coal	500.6(B2) p.372
Coat of plaster, heating cables	424.41(C) p.299
Coating processes	Art. 516 p.434
Coaxial cable grounding cond.,	820.100(A3) p.689
Coaxial cable separation lightning	820.44(F3) p.688
Coaxial cable, conductive shield	820.93(A) p.688
Coaxial cable, exposed to lightning	820.93 p.688
Coaxial cable, low energy power	820.15 p.687
Coaxial cable, sep. from class 1	820.133(A2) p.692
Coaxial cables buried, separation	820.47(B) p.688
Coaxial cables, fire minimum size	760.49(A) p.653
Coaxial cables, steel center cond.	760.179(H) p.659
Code arrangement	90.3 p.23
Code enforcement, inspector	90.4 p.23

Entry	Reference
Code letter, motor	T.430.7(B) p.313
Coefficient of expansion	300.7(B) I.N. p.140
Coke dust	500.6(B2) p.372
Cold-storage warehouses, fixtures	410.10(A) p.281
Collect deposits in ducts or hoods	410.10(C3) p.281
Collector rings, definition	675.2 p.573
Collector rings, open motors	430.14(B) p.316
Collector rings, revolving machines	490.54 p.365
Color braid of flexible cords	400.22(A) p.261
Color isolated conductors	517.160(A5) p.457
Color, blue	504.80(C) p.397
Color, blue 208v heat cable	424.35 p.298
Color, brown 277v heat cable	424.35 p.298
Color, brown isolated conductor	517.160(A5) p.457
Color, gray	200.7 p.47
Color, gray	200.6 p.46
Color, gray	400.22(A&C) p.261
Color, gray	200.7(C3) I.N. p.47
Color, green	250.119 p.123
Color, green	250.119(C) p.123
Color, green	250.126 p.125
Color, green	310.110(B) p.172
Color, green	400.23(B) p.261
Color, green	550.16 p.486
Color, light blue	504.80(C) p.397
Color, light blue, cords	400.22(C) p.261
Color, orange	110.15 p.36
Color, orange	230.56 p.84
Color, orange isolated conductor	517.160(A5) p.457
Color, red 240v heat cable	424.35 p.298
Color, white	200.6(A1) p.46
Color, white	200.6(A1) p.46
Color, white	200.7 p.47
Color, white	400.22(A&C) p.261
Color, yellow 120v heat cable	424.35 p.298
Colored braid, flexible cords	400.22(A) p.261
Colored stripe	200.6(A1) p.46
Colors, branch circuits	210.5 p.49
Colors, conductors	310.110 p.172
Colors, heating cables	424.35 p.298
Column-width panelboard	300.3(B4) p.135
Combustible carbonaceous dust	500.6(B2) p.372
Combustible dust Class II location	500.5(C) p.370
Combustible dust	506.2 p.412
Combustible fibers Class III Div.2	500.5(D) p.371
Combustible material, fixture	410.115(A) p.286
Combustible shades, fixtures	410.70 p.285
Combustible walls front edge of box	314.20 p.180
Commercial cooking equipment	T.220.56 p.67
Commercial cooking hood	410.10(C1) p.281
Commercial garages Class I Div.2	511.3 p.420
Commercial garages GFCI	511.12 p.422
Commercial garages pit air changes	511.3(D1) p.420
Commissioning tests	708.8 p.637
Common grounding electrode	250.58 p.113
Common neutral	225.7(B) p.71
Common-return conductors,	650.8 p.565
Communication circuits, lightning	800.53 p.672
Communication cond. pole spacing	800.44(A1) p.671
Communication cond., spacing	225.14(D) p.72
Communication cts., grounding	800.100(B2) p.674
Communication systems, broadband	Art. 840 p.707
Communication wires	800.179 p.680
Communication wires, seperation	800.133 p.677
Communication wires, voltage rating	800.179 p.680
Communication, equipment	90.2(B4) p.22
Communications circuits	Art. 800 p.669
Communications, bonding elect.	800.100(D) p.674
Communications, cabled outlet	800.156 p.678
Communications, electrode	800.100(B) p.674
Communications, grd. conductor	800.100(A3) p.673
Communications, point of entry	800.47 p.671
Community antenna grd. elect.	820.100(A3) p.689
Community antenna TV and radio	Art. 820 p.686
Commutators open motors	430.14(B) p.316
Compact aluminum conductor	Table 5(A) p.720
Compacted strands	501.15 I.N. #2 p.377
Compactor, cord length	422.16(B2) p.292
Compatible with the charger	700.12(A) p.625
Compensate for voltage drop	250.122(B) p.124
Completed seal, thickness	501.15(C3) p.379
Composition bushing	300.4(G) p.137
Compound, sealing thickness	501.15(C3) p.379
Computed floor area lighting load	220.12 p.61
Computer room data process I.T.E.	645.4 I.N. p.561
Computer room, fire cable	645.5(D6) p.561
Computer systems neutral	210.4(A) I.N. p.48
Concentric knockouts, bonding	250.97 ex. p.118
Concentricity	T.400.4 note 7 p.257
Concrete embedded elements	547.10(A1&2) p.480
Concrete or wood above raceway	390.3(A) p.238
Concrete, brick or tile grounded	T.110.26(A1) p.38
Concrete-encased electrode	250.52(A3) p.112
Concretetight type fittings	342.42 p.203
Cond. nipple, no derating	T.310.15B(3)(2) p.152
Cond. seals, pressurized enclosure	501.15(A2) p.378
Condensation, foreign systems	110.26(E1b) p.39
Condominiums, boat	555.1 p.513
Conduct safely any ground fault	250.96(A) p.118
Conductive materials ground	250.4(A2) p.101
Conductive reinforcing wire	668.31 p.571
Conductive surfaces	424.41(H) p.299
Conductive, optical fiber cables	770.2 p.660
Conductor insul., stage lights	520.42 p.462

Conductor insulation, batteries	625.17 p.545
Conductor minimum size, fixture	402.6 p.266
Conductor to be grounded AC	250.26 p.106
Conductor, bending radius hi-volt	300.34 p.145
Conductor, support spacing	T.300.19(A) p.143
Conductor, supports	398.30 p.249
Conductors #8 & larger stranded	310.106(C) p.172
Conductors #8 & larger, supports	398.30(B) p.249
Conductors are laid in place	376.2 p.230
Conductors entering a building	300.5(D2) p.139
Conductors for portables	520.68 p.467
Conductors in manholes	110.74 p.45
Conductors in raceways	300.17 p.142
Conductors of the same circuit	300.3(B) p.135
Conductors, 60° C	110.14(C1A) p.36
Conductors, 75° C	110.14(C1A2) p.36
Conductors, AC-DC same conduit	300.3(C1) p.136
Conductors, adjacent load-carry	310.15(A3)(4) p.150
Conductors, aluminum size	310.106(B) p.171
Conductors, antenna clearance	810.54 p.685
Conductors, arc projector	540.13 p.477
Conductors, bare	310.15(B3) p.152
Conductors, braided-covered	300.39 p.145
Conductors, bridge wire	610.21(D) p.530
Conductors, bundled	T.310.15(B2a) p.150
Conductors, buried minimum cover	T.300.5 p.138
Conductors, cell line	668.12 p.570
Conductors, Class 1 circuit	725.2 p.641
Conductors, common return	650.6(C) p.565
Conductors, considered outside	230.6 p.79
Conductors, contact installation	610.21 p.530
Conductors, controllers, resistors	430.32(E) p.320
Conductors, copper-clad Alum.	T.310.15(B)(16)p.154
Conductors, corrosive conditions	310.10(G) p.148
Conductors, different insulations	310.10 p.147
Conductors, direct burial	310.10(F) p.148
Conductors, dissimilar metals	110.14 p.36
Conductors, electroplating	669.5 p.571
Conductors, emerging from ground	300.5(D1) p.139
Conductors, fire circuits	760.49 p.653
Conductors, free air	T.310.15(B)(17) p.155
Conductors, grounding size	T. 250.122 p.125
Conductors, grouped together	300.20(A) p.144
Conductors, heat dissipates	310.15(A3)(3) p.150
Conductors, heat generated	310.15(A3)(2) p.150
Conductors, identification	310.110 p.172
Conductors, in parallel	310.10(H) p.148
Conductors, less than 50v	720.4 p.640
Conductors, low & high voltage	300.32 p. 145
Conductors, marker tape	310.120(B2) p.173
Conductors, marking requirement	310.120 p.173
Conductors, methods of const.	310.104 p.168
Conductors, minimum size	T.310.106 p.171
Conductors, nonshielded	310.10(E) p.148
Conductors, number and size	300.17 p.142
Conductors, oil resistant	T.310.104(A) p.168
Conductors, on poles supports	225.14(D) p.72
Conductors, open service	T.230.51(C) p.83
Conductors, operating temperature	310.10 p.147
Conductors, organs	650.5(C) p.564
Conductors, outdoor overhead over 600v	Art. 399 p.250
Conductors, outside a building	230.6 p.79
Conductors, overhead pool	680.8 p.577
Conductors, ozone resistant	310.10(E) p.148
Conductors, pilot lights	520.53(G) p.464
Conductors, power-limit. fire	760.46 p.653
Conductors, racked up	110.74 p.45
Conductors, service entrance size	230.42 p.82
Conductors, shielding	310.10(E) p.148
Conductors, solid dielectric	310.10(E) p.148
Conductors, stranded #8 in raceway	310.106(C) p.172
Conductors, stranded on fixt.chain	410.56(E) p.284
Conductors, suffixes marking	310.120(C) p.173
Conductors, supp. vert. raceways	300.19 p.143
Conductors, support methods	300.19(B) p.143
Conductors, surface marking	310.120(B1) p.173
Conductors, tag marking	310.120(B3) p.173
Conductors, temp. limitations	310.10 p.147
Conductors, to be grounded	250.26 p.106
Conductors, wet locations	310.10(C) p.148
Conductors, within 3" of ballast	410.68 p.285
Conductors, Xenon projectors	540.13 p.477
Conductors, X-ray equipment	660.6 p.566
Conduit bodies, accessible	314.29 p.184
Conduit bodies, cross-section area	314.16(C1) p.178
Conduit bodies, seals Class I Div.1	501.15(A1) p.377
Conduit nipple, fill 60%	Chapter 9 note 4 p.671
Conduit stems Class I Div.1	501.130(A3) p.384
Conduit, bend radius	Chapter 9 Table 2 p.711
Conduit, burial depth	T.300.5 p.138
Conduit, cutting die 3/4"	334.28 p.204
Conduit, fill percent	Table 1 p.711
Conduit, fill percent	Table 4 p.712
Conduit, HDPE size	353.20(B) p.211
Conduit, IMC, taper per foot	342.28 p.202
Conduit, rigid, taper per foot	344.28 p.204
Conduit, romex fill%	Table 1 p.711
Conduit, seals Class I, Div.1	501.15(A1) p.377
Conduit, seals Class I, Div.2	501.15(B2) p.378
Conduit, support of cables	300.11(B) p.141
Conduits, two or more in box	314.23(E) p.181
Connected conductors	110.14(C) *I.N.* p.36
Connecting cables, data	645.5(C) p.561
Connection ahead of disconnect	700.12 p.624

Connection to terminals	230.81 p.85	Coordination, electrical system	240.12 p.92
Connector strips, stage	520.46 p.463	Coordination, emergency O.C.P.	700.27 p.627
Considered as alive	410.140(C) p.288	Copper bars, ampacity	366.23(A) p.223
Considered as energized	410.130(B) p.286	Copper conductors	110.5 p.35
Consignee yards, truck	626.2 I.N. p.547	Copper conductors minimum size	T.310.106(A)p.172
Construction sites GFCI	590.6 p.518	Copper conductors, control circuit	430.9(B) p.314
Construction sites, multiwire cts.	590.4(D) p.517	Copper protector grd. conductor	800.100(A2) p.673
Contact conductors installation	610.21 p.530	Copper-clad Alum.	T.310.15(B)(16) p.154
Contact with bodies, volts	517.64(A1) p.455	COPS	Art. 708 p.635
Contaminants, motors	430.13 p.315	Cord & plug connect. arc welder	210.21(B) ex.2 p.54
Contaminated by foreign materials	110.12(B) p.35	Cord bushings, fixtures	410.84 p.285
Contiguous with hospitals	517.40(C) p.450	Cord connector, cord pendant	210.50(A) p.55
Contiguous, underfloor raceways	390.3(B) p.238	Cord connectors and receptacles	406.7 p.272
Continuity of the circuitry	410.155(B) p.289	Cord length, air conditioner	440.64 p.346
Continuity, bonding concentric KO	250.92(B) p.117	Cord length, compactors	422.16(B2) p.292
Continuity, clean surfaces	250.12 p.103	Cord length, dishwasher	422.16(B2) p.292
Continuity, device removal	300.13(B) p.141	Cord length, fountain	680.51(E) p.588
Continuity, equip. grd. conductor	250.124 p.124	Cord length, pool	680.7 p.577
Continuity, mechanical	300.12 p.141	Cord length, waste disposers	422.16(B1) p.292
Continuous amps exceed 3 times	240.101(A) p.100	Cord listing	240.5 p.90
Continuous between cabinets	300.12 p.141	Cord pendants	314.23(H) p.181
Continuous duty, escalator	620.61(B2) p.542	Cord pendants, receptacle outlet	210.50(A) p.55
Continuous duty, motors	T.430.22(E) p.317	Cord polarity, appliances	422.40 p.294
Continuous industrial process	230.95 ex. p.87	Cord, range hood	422.16(B4) p. 293
Continuous load, branch circuit	210.19(A1) p.52	Cord, strain relief, mobile homes	550.10(B) p.482
Continuous load, feeders	215.2(A) p.59	Cord-connected showcases	410.59 p.284
Continuous load, services	230.42(A1) p.82	Cords & cables for border lights	520.44(C) p.462
Continuous-duty F.L.C. rating	440.41(B) p.345	Cords, all elastomer	T.400.4 p.255
Control & signal elev. cable note 7	T.400.4 p.251	Cords, all plastic parallel	T.400.4 p.255
Control circuit devices torque	430.9(C) p.314	Cords, ampacity	T.400.5(A)(1) p.258
Control circuit devices, copper cond	430.9(B) p.314	Cords, appliances	422.16 p.292
Control circuit overcurrent protect.	725.43 p.642	Cords, attachment plugs	400.7(B) p.260
Control drawing, intrinsically safe	504.10(A) p.395	Cords, colored braid	400.22(A) p.261
Control instruments, connect.	501.105(B6) p.382	Cords, colored insulation	400.22(C) p.261
Control panel, duty cycle	409.20 p. 278	Cords, colored separator	400.22(D) p.261
Control panel, industrial	409.2 p. 278	Cords, cooking units	422.16(B3) p.292
Control relative humidity	424.38(C) p.299	Cords, ease in servicing	422.16(B3) p.292
Control transformer, motors	430.75(B) p.327	Cords, extra hard usage	502.140 p.390
Controlled vented power fuse	DEF. 100 p.34	Cords, extra-hard usage	410.62(B) p.284
Converter, rec. vehicle	551.2 p.490	Cords, extra-hard usage	410.62(B) p.284
Conveyors or hangers, support	516.10(4) p.438	Cords, extreme flexibility	T.400.4 note 4 p.257
Convolutions, thread into	348.28 p.206	Cords, fountain length	680.51(E) p.588
Cooking equip., neutral B.C.	210.19(A3) ex 2 p.53	Cords, hard service	T.400.4 p.253
Cooking units, cord connected	422.16(B3) p.292	Cords, hard usage for fixtures	410.62(B) p.284
Cooktops, feeder demand	T.220.55 p.66	Cords, heater	T.400.4 p.252
Cooling, of equipment	110.13(B) p.35	Cords, in show windows	400.11 p.260
Coordinated O.C.P.	110.10 p.35	Cords, jacketed tinsel	T.400.4 p.257
Coordinated therm.overload	T.450.3(B) note 3 p.349	Cords, junior hard service	T.400.4 p.254
Coordinated	700.27 p. 627	Cords, knotting	400.10 I.N. p.260
Coordinated, temperature limit.	110.14(C) p.36	Cords, labels	400.20 p.260
Coordination	240.12 p.92	Cords, lamp	T.400.4 p.251
Coordination selective	DEF 100 p.27	Cords, length pool	680.7(A) p.577

Cords, marking	400.6 p.259	Cranes, protected by fuse & C.B.	610.42(A) p.531
Cords, minimum size	400.21 p.261	Crawl space equipment	210.63 p.58
Cords, overcurrent protection	240.5 p.90	Crawl spaces, GFCI	210.8(A4) p.50
Cords, overcurrent protection	400.13 p.260	Critical branch, definition	517.1 p.440
Cords, parallel heater	T.400.4 p.252	Critical care area receptacles	517.19(B) p.444
Cords, parallel tinsel	T.400.4 p.256	Critical Operations Power Systems	Art. 708 p.635
Cords, pendants	400.7(A1) p.260	Crossarms, communication cts.	800.44(A2) p.671
Cords, plugging boxes	530.18(E) p.474	Cross-connect arrays	800.110(I) p.676
Cords, protection from damage	400.14 p.260	Crossings, FCC	324.18 p.189
Cords, room air conditioner	440.64 p.346	Cross-sectional area	Table 4 100% p.712
Cords, shall not be concealed	400.8(5) p.260	Crowfeet, fixtures	410.36(C) p.283
Cords, showcase	410.59 p.284	Crucibles, definition	668.2 p.569
Cords, sign	600.10(C1) p.522	CSA, cross-section area	Table 4 100% p.712
Cords, splices not permitted	400.9 p.260	Cupboards	210.52(3) p.55
Cords, strain or physical damage	410.62(B) p.284	Curing apparatus required outlets	516.3(F) p.436
Cords, surface marking	400.22(F) p.261	Current collectors Class III	503.155(C) p.394
Cords, tension	400.10 p.260	Current rating of the unit, fixture	410.74(B) p.285
Cords, theater stages	T.400.4 note 6 p.257	Current sensing device	669.9(2) p.572
Cords, tinned conductors	400.22(E) p.261	Current transformers, cases	250.172 ex. p.129
Cords, TPT, TST types	T.400.4 note 4 p.257	Current-limiting O.C.P. device	240.2 p.89
Cords, tracer in braid	400.22(B) p.261	Curtain machines, stage	520.48 p.463
Cords, twisted portable	T.400.4 p.253	Cut or abrade the insulation	410.56(A) p.283
Cords, use of sound recording	640.42 p.559	Cutout boxes wet location	312.2 p.174
Cords, uses not permitted	400.8 p.260	Cutout boxes, plugs or plates	110.12(A) p.35
Cords, uses permitted	400.7 p.260	Cutouts and fuse links	490.21(C) p.362
Cords, vacuum cleaner	T.400.4 p.256	Cutouts, flashers signs	600.6(B) p.520
Cords, winding with tape	400.10 *I.N.* p.260	Cutting die, conduit	342.28 p.202
Corner-grounded delta	240.85 p.97	Cutting die, conduit	344.28 p.204
Corner-grounded delta	250.20 *I.N.* p.104	Cutting die, conduit	500.8(E) p.375
Corrosion, deteriorating agent	110.11 p.35	Cutting slots in metal	300.20(B) p.144
Corrosion-resistant NMC cable	334.10(B) p.196	Cutting tables, lampholders	530.41 p.475
Corrosion-resistant UF cable	340.116 p.202	Cyclic operation, heat	424.22(D3) p.298
Corrosive atmosphere	547.5(C3) p.479		
Counter top receptacles	210.52(C) p. 56		
Counter top surfaces	210.8(A6) p.50	-D-	
Counter-mount. cook. recpts.	210.52(B2) ex.2 p.56		
Counters, bar type recpts. required	210.52(A2)(3)p.56		
Cove lighting, adequate space	410.18 p.281	Dairies, indoor wet locations	300.6(D) p.140
Cover, boxes	314.25 p.182	Damage to conductors	300.17 p.142
Cover, buried cable definition	T.300.5 Note 1 p.138	Dampers, transformers	450.45(E) p.355
Cover, faceplate or canopy	314.25 p.182	Damping means, motors	430.52(3) *I.N.* p.323
Cover, gutter	366.100(D) p.224	Damping transitory overvoltages	450.5(C) p.350
Cover, hi-voltage in concrete	300.50(2) p.146	Dance halls, place of assembly	518.2 p.458
Covers, manhole	110.75(D) p. 45	Danger High Voltage	490.53 p.365
Crane or hoist, more than 1 motor	610.14(E) p.528	Danger-High Voltage-Keep out	110.34(C) p.43
Crane rail as conductor	610.21(F4) p.530	Dangerous temperature	240.1 *I.N.* p.89
Crane-runway track	610.21(F4) p.530	Dangerous temperatures	240.100(C) p.100
Cranes Class III location	250.22(1) p.104	Data errors, grounding	250.6(D) p.103
Cranes & hoists	Art. 610 p.527	Data processing rooms, disconnect	645.10 p.562
Cranes & monorail hoists, locked open	610.32 p.531	Data processing, branch circuits	645.5(A) p.561
Cranes or hoists, demand fact.	T.610.14(E) p.530	Datum plane	555.2 p.513
Cranes, bridge wire contact conduct.	610.21(D) p.530	Datum plane GFCI	682.15 p. 592

DC cell line, process power supply	668.11 p.569	Demand factor, shore power recpts.	555.12 p.513
DC circuits, 3-wire	240.15(B4) p.92	Demand factor, small appliances	T.220.42 p.64
DC conductors for electroplating	669.9 p.572	Dentist office, alternate power	517.44(B) p.452
DC generators, protection	530.63 p.475	Depot facilities, truck	626.2 *I.N.* p.547
DC Motor, FLC	T.430.247 p.336	Derangement, emergency systems	700.7(A) p.623
DC plugging boxes	530.14 p.473	Derating factors trench cond.	310.15(B3)(3) p.152
DC resistance,	Table 8 p.721	Design, specification	90.1(C) p.22
DC system grounding	685.12 p.593	Designated Critical Operations Areas	708.2DEF p.636
DCOA	708.1 p.636	Destructive corrosive conditions	330.12 p.193
Dead end open wiring	398.30(A2) p.249	Deter access	110.31 p.40
Dead ends nonmetallic wireway	378.58 p.232	Deteriorating agent	110.11 p.35
Dead ends, wireways	376.58 p.231	Device box, double volume	314.16(B4) p.178
Dead front, panelboard	408.38 p.276	Device removal, continuity	300.13(B) p.141
Dead-front & dead-rear	520.24 p.461	Device wider than 2"	314.16(B4) p.178
Dead-front construction, plugs	406.7(A) p.272	Device, entertainment	522.2DEF p.468
Decimal fraction .8	Table 1 note 7 p.711	Devices of insulating material	334.40(B) p.198
Decorative bands, fixtures	410.42 p.283	Devices rated 800 amps or less	240.4(B) p.90
Decorative lighting outfits	410.54(B) p.283	Devices rated over 800 amps	240.4(C) p.90
Decorative panels	424.42 p.299	Devices, strike termination	250.53(B) p.112
Dedicated electrical space, indoors	110.26(E1A) p.39	Devices, strike termination	250.60 p.113
Dedicated equipment space	110.26(E) p.39	Diagnostic equipment	517.73(A) p.455
Dedicated space, panelboard	110.26(E) p.39	Diagnostic equipment, O.C.P.	517.73(A) p.455
Dedicated space, sprinkler protect.	110.26(E1c) p.39	Diagrams, feeder	215.5 p.60
Definition unfinished basement	210.8(A5) p.50	Diameter rods, gas cable	T.326.116 p.192
Deflecting the cables	300.19(C3) p.144	Dielectric constant	517.160(A6) p.457
Deformed at normal temp.	310.104 p.168	Dielectric fluid, transformers	450.24 p.353
Degree of flexibility	356.30(2) p.217	Dielectric heating definition	665.2 p.567
Dehydrate, Organic dust	500.8(D2) p.375	Dielectric strength test	550.17 p.487
De-icing equipment	Art. 426 p.304	Diesel engine as prime mover	700.12(B2) p.625
Deleterious effect	310.10(G) p.148	Different circuits in same cable	725.136(B) p.645
Deleteriously affected, bushing	445.16 p.347	Different circuits same cable	725.48 p.643
Delta breakers	408.36(C) p.276	Different intrinsically safe circuits	504.2 *I.N. #1* p.394
Delta high-leg, feeder	110.15 p.36	Different potential	230.54(E) p.84
Delta high-leg, panelboard	408.3(E) p. 274	Different rate schedules	230.2(D) p.79
Delta high-leg, service	230.56 p.84	Different volt., freq., phases, feeders	225.30(D) p.74
Delta, phase arrangement	408.3(E) p.274	Different volt., freq., phases, svcs.	230.2(D) p.79
Demarcation, point of DEF 100 service point	*I.N.* p.32	Diffraction and irradiation types	660.23(B) p.566
Demand factor,	DEF 100 p.28	Diffusers, thermal shock	410.10(C2) p.281
Demand factor, cooking equip.	T.220.55 p.66	Dimmer systems 3-phase, 4-wire	518.5 p.459
Demand factor, dryers	T.220.54 p.65	Dimmers, autotransformer	520.25(C) p.461
Demand factor, elevators	T.620.14 p.536	Dimmers, night club	520.25(A) p.461
Demand factor, farm	T.220.102&103 p.70	Dimmers, overcurrent protection	520.25(A) p.461
Demand factor, fixed appliances	220.53 p.65	Dining facilities	518.2(A) p.458
Demand factor, kitchen equip.	T.220.56 p.67	Dipping processes	Art. 516 p.434
Demand factor, laundry	T.220.42 p.64	Direct burial conductors	310.10(F) p.148
Demand factor, lighting	T.220.42 p.64	Direct burial S loops	300.5(J) *I.N.* p.139
Demand factor, mobile homes	T.550.31 p.489	Direct burial, raceway transitions	300.5(J) *I.N.* p.139
Demand factor, optional DW unit	220.82 p.67	Direct buried cable, splices, & taps	300.5(E) p.139
Demand factor, optional DW units	T.220.84 p.69	Direct current switchbrds, motion pict.	530.64 p.475
Demand factor, optional restaurant	T.220.88 p.70	Direct grade level access	210.52(E1) p.57
Demand factor, optional school	T.220.86 p.69	Direction & elevations of runs	392.100(E) p.246
Demand factor, receptacles	220.44 p.64	Directional boring equipment, approved	300.5(K) p.139

Tom Henry's KEY WORD INDEX

Directional boring	300.5(K) p.139	Display pools, fountains	680.2 p.576
Directional sign disconnect	600.6 ex. p.520	Disposers, cord length	422.16(B1)(2) p.292
Directories of electrical	300.21 *I.N.* p.144	Dissimilar loads	220.60 p.65
Directory of circuits, panelboard	110.22 p.37	Dissimilar metals	358.12(6) p.218
Directory, or plaque	225.37 p.75	Dissimilar metals, alum. & steel	344.14 p.204
Directory, or plaque	230.2(E) p.79	Dissimilar metals, conductors of	110.14 p.36
Disc. means, firepumps, feeder	225.34(B) p.75	Dissipation of heat	300.17 p.142
Discharge lighting over 1000v	410.140(A) p.288	Distinctive marking	200.6(A1) p.46
Disconecting means, phase converter	455.20 p.356	Distinctive marking, terminals	200.10(A) p.47
Disconnect means, occupant access	225.35 p.75	Distributing frames	T.800.154(A) p.679
Disconnect, A/C	440.11 p.342	Distribution apparatus	250.110 ex.2 p.121
Disconnect, amp rating, motor	430.110(A) p.332	Distribution cutouts	490.21(C) p.362
Disconnect, appliances	422.31(A) p.293	Distribution system mobile home	550.30 p.489
Disconnect, computer/data	645.10 p.562	Distribution systems, yard and pier	555.4 p.513
Disconnect, dispensing pump	514.11 p.428	Divided equally, track loads	210.11(B) p.51
Disconnect, elevator	620.51 p.540	Docks, Class I location	513.4(B) p.423
Disconnect, heat	424.19 p.296	Documented hazardous area	500.4(A) p.368
Disconnect, heating assemblies	427.55(B) p.310	Does not carry the main power	430.2 DEF p.311
Disconnect, high-voltage	230.205 p.88	Domed covers	314.16(A) p.178
Disconnect, hook sticks bus bar	368.17(C) p.225	Domestic oil burner	430.32(B3) p.320
Disconnect, irrigation machines	675.8 p.574	Donut-type current trans.	450.5(A3) *I.N.* p.350
Disconnect, locked-rotor	430.110(C1) p.332	Door bell wiring, Class 2	725.121(A5) p.644
Disconnect, marked indicate purpose	110.22(A) p.37	Door bell wiring, same raceway w/power	725.136(A) p.645
Disconnect, mobile homes	550.11(A) p.483	Door vehicle, attached garage	210.70(A2) p.58
Disconnect, motors	430.101 p.330	Doors, personnel	110.26(C3) p.39
Disconnect, outbuildings snap sw.	225.36 ex. p.75	Double ended	250.24(A3) p.105
Disconnect, outline lighting	600.6 p.520	Double insulated	250.114 ex. p.121
Disconnect, range	422.33(B) p.293	Double locknuts	501.30(A) p.381
Disconnect, self-service station	514.11(A) p.428	Double-coil circuit breaker	445.12(E) p.347
Disconnect, service maximum	230.71(A) p.84	Double-pole switched lampholder	410.93 p.285
Disconnect, sign	600.6 p.520	Downspout, outdoors	225.6(B) p.71
Disconnect, snap switch	225.36 ex. p.75	DP cable	645.5(E6) p.561
Disconnect, welder arc	630.13 p.553	Draglines over 600v	490.51(A) p.365
Disconnect, welder resistance	630.33 p.554	Drain fittings	680.43(D4) ex.1 p.587
Disconnect, X-ray equipment	660.5 p.566	Drainage of raceways	225.22 p.73
Disconnecting link, busways	368.239 p.226	Drainage of raceways	230.53 p.83
Disconnecting means location, feeder	225.32 p.74	Draining charge, capacitor	460.6 p.357
Disconnecting means marked	110.22 p.37	Drawbridges	T.430.22(E) p.317
Disconnecting means type	430.109 p.331	Draw-out type switchgear	490.22 p.363
Disconnecting means, snap switch	225.36 p.75	Dredges over 600v	490.51(A) p.365
Disconnecting motors & controllers	430.101 p.330	Dressing room, pilot light	520.73 p.468
Disconnecting ungrounded conductors	225.31 p.74	Dressing rooms, lights & recpts.	520.73 p.468
Disconnection of photovoltaic equip.	690.15 p.600	Drinking water coolers	440.13 p.343
Discontinued outlets	374.7 p.229	Drip loops	230.52 p.83
Discontinued outlets	390.8 p.239	Drip loops, services	230.54(F) p.84
Dishes, antennas	810.16(B) p.683	Dripproof, enclosures tunnels	110.59 p.44
Dishwasher, cord length	422.16(B2)(2) p.292	Drive system, adjustable speed	430.122(A) p.333
Dishwasher, wire size	T.310.106(A) p.172	Drivers, LED	220.18(B) p.64
Dishwasher, wire size	210.23(A) p.54	Driveways, service height	230.24(B) p.80
Dishwashers, rec. vehicle	551.2 *I.N.* p.490	Driving machine motors	620.61(B3) p.542
Disinfecting agents, flammable	517.60(A2) p.453	Drop boxes, stage	520.46 p.463
Dispensing pump, disconnect	514.11(A) p.428	Dropped ceilings	110.26(E1d) p.39

Dry board installations	424.41(G) p.299	Egress lighting, thermal protection	410.130(E4) p.287
Dry cell battery, limited power	725.121(A5) p.644	Egress, from working space	110.26(C3) p.39
Dry kraft paper tapes	326.112 p.191	Egress, illumination	517.42(A) p.451
Dryer, clothes washer	Example D2b p.805	Either side of the boundary	501.15(B2) p.378
Dryer, minimum load	220.54 p.65	Ejector mechanisms, plugs	406.6(C) p.272
Dryer, neutral	220.61(B1) p.67	Elbow, metal grounding	250.86 ex. 3 p.117
Dryer, use nameplate load	220.84(C3) p.69	Elbows capped	314.16(C)(3) p.179
Dryers, household	220.54 p.65	Electric arc flash hazards	110.16 p.37
Drying apparatus	516.3(F) p.436	Electric cranes grounding	250.22 p.104
Dry-niche fixture, definition	680.2 p.575	Electric discharge light. trans.	600.21(A) p.522
Drywall, repairing	314.21 p.180	Electric discharge lighting	410.140(A) p.288
Dual fuel supplies emergency	700.12(B3) p.625	Electric discharge tubing	600.41 p.524
Duct heaters	424.57 p.300	Electric furnace transformer	450.26 ex.3 p.353
Duct work, heaters	424.12(B) p.296	Electric furnaces	250.21(1) p.104
Ducts, electrical	310.2 DEF p.147	Electric heat, disconnect	424.19 p.296
Ducts or plenums wiring methods	300.22(B) p.144	Electric heat, unit switch	424.19(C) p.297
Ducts to transport dust	300.22(A) p.144	Electric heating, branch circuit	424.3 p.296
Ducts, type BLP	830.179(B1) p.705	Electric mixer	501.140(A4) p.385
Ducts, wiring in	300.22 p.144	Electric signs	600 p.519
Dumbwaiter,	DEF 100 Hoistway p.29	Electric space heating, outlets	424.3(A) p.296
Dumbwaiters	620 p.532	Electric supply company	230.204(D) p.88
Dump load, Definition	694.2 p.610	Electric systems, small wind	Art. 694 p.610
Dust with water, excessive	547.1(A) p.478	Electric vehicle charging	511.10(B) p. 422
Dust, aluminum	500.6(B1) I.N. p.372	Electric vehicle coupler, DEF	625.2 p.543
Dust, combustible Class II location	500.5(C) p.370	Electric vehicle inlet, DEF	625.2 p.544
Dust, magnesium	500.6(B1) I.N. p.372	Electric vehicle polarization	625.9(A) p.544
Dust, transformer or capacitor	502.100(A3) p.388	Electric vehicle supply cable, length	625.17 p.545
Duty cycle, control panel	409.20 p. 278	Electric vehicle supply equip.	625.13 p.544
Dwelling example,	p.804	Electric vehicle ventilation	625.29(C & D) p.546
Dwelling service size	T.310.15(B7) p.153	Electric welders, insulation of conduct.	630.41 p.554
Dwelling, light circuit voltage	210.6(A1) p.49	Electric welders, marking	630.14 p.553
Dwellings, over 1000v lighting	410.140(A) p. 288	Electrical components, heaters	424.12(B) p.296
Dwellings, receptacles *no limit	220.14(J) p.63	Electrical contact	250.110(3) p.121
Dynamic braking resistor	430.29 p.318	Electrical continuity, cable tray	392.18(A) p.240
		Electrical continuity, FCC cable	324.40(A) p. 189
		Electrical continuity, services	250.92(B) p.117
		Electrical cranes Class III location	250.22(1) p.104
		Electrical datum plane	555.2 p.513
		Electrical datum plane	682.2 DEF p. 591
-E-		Electrical ducts	310.60(A) p.158
Earth resistivity	800.90(A) I.N. #(2) & #(3) p.672	Electrical ducts, Definition	310.2 p.147
Earth, equipment grd. conductor	250.54 p.113	Electrical equipment, space	110.26(A3) p.38
Earth, movement	300.5(J) p.139	Electrical inspection, qualifications	80.27 p.826
Ease in servicing, cords	422.16(B3) p.292	Electrical inspector, chief, definition	80.2 p.821
Easily ignitible fibers	500.5(D) p.371	Electrical life support	DEF 517.2 p.440
Easily ignitible material	240.24(D) p.95	Electrical metallic tubing (EMT)	358.1 p. 218
Eccentric knockouts	250.92(B) p.117	Electrical nameplates	550.11(D) p.484
Effective continuity between enclose	250.96(A) p.118	Electrical noise	250.146(D) p.127
Effective ground fault	250.4(5) p.101	Electrical noise, receptacles	406.3(D) p.270
Effective grounding path	250.68(B) p.116	Electrical nonmetallic tubing	362.2 p.220
Effective interlocks	516.3(F) p.436	Electrical permits, issuance	80.19(C) p.824
Egress lighting energized	410.130(E4) p.287	Electrical potential to bodies	517.64(A1) p.455
Egress lighting, emergency	700.16 p.626		

Electrical rating, fixture	410.74(B) p.285
Electrically cond. compound	300.6(A) p.139
Electrically connected,	DEF 668.2 p.569
Electrically continuous, grounding	250.64(E) p.114
Electrically driven machines grd.	675.13 p.575
Electrically heated appl. signal	422.42 p.294
Electrically heated appliances	422.43(A) p.294
Electric-disc. light 1000v or less	410.130 p.286
Electric-discharge lamp	410.104(A) p.286
Electrified truck parking spaces	Art. 626 p.547
Electrocuted, health care	517.11 I.N. p.443
Electrode, communications	800.100(B) p.674
Electrode, diameter	250.52(5B) p.112
Electrode, plate 2 sq.ft.	250.52(7) p.112
Electrodes, grounding	250.52(5A) p.112
Electrodes, nonferrous thickness	250.52(7) p.112
Electrode-type boilers	424.80 p.301
Electroendosmosis	310.104 I.N. p.168
Electrolysis of the sheath	110.36 p.43
Electrolyte, batteries	480.8(B) p.360
Electrolytic cell definition	668.2 p.569
Electrolytic cell lines	668.3(C) p.569
Electromagnetic interference	250.146(D) p.127
Electromagnetic interference, jack	517.2 DEF p.442
Electromagnetic valve supply	650.6(A) p.565
Electronic cameras	530.1 p.472
Electronic equip., isolated grd.	250.96(B) p.118
Electronic organs, sound	640.1 p.554
Electronically actuated fuse	DEF 100 p.33
Electroplating	Art. 669 p.571
Electroplating, overcurrent prot.	669.9 p.572
Electrostatic air cleaner	422.12 ex. p.292
Electrostatic equipment	516.10(A2) p.438
Electrostatic equipment	516.10(B4) p.439
Electrostatic fluidized beds	516.10(C4) p.439
Electrostatic shield	517.160(A2) p.457
Electrostatic spray zones, signs	516.10A(8) p.438
Electrostatic spraying	516.10(A) p.438
Electrostatically charged	516.10(A) p.438
Elevation of live parts	T.110.34(E) p.43
Elevator cable	T.400.4 p.251
Elevator car	620.41 I.N. p.539
Elevator car tops	620.85 p.543
Elevator car, AC branch circuit	620.3(C) p.533
Elevator disconnect location	620.51(C) p.540
Elevator disconnecting means	620.51(D) p.541
Elevator driving machine	620.51(D) p.541
Elevator machine room, receptacles	620.23(C) p.538
Elevator system, regenerate power	620.91(A) p.543
Elevator traveling cables	T.400.4 note 7 p.257
Elevator, car lights	620.22(A) p.538
Elevators	Art. 620 p.532
Elevators, conductors	620.11 p.534
Elevators, demand factors	T.620.14 p.536
Elevators, door interlock wiring	620.11(A) p.534
Elevators, emergency power	620.91 p.543
Elevators, GFCI	620.85 p.543
Elevators, grounding	620.81 p.543
Elevators, lighting parallel	620.12(A1) p.535
Elevators, machine room	620.71 p.542
Elevators, other bldg. loads	620.91(B) p.543
Elevators, regenerated power	620.91(A) p.543
Elevators, travel. cables	T.400.4 note 7 p.257
Elevators, traveling cables	620.12(A1) p.535
Elliptical cross section	Table 1 note 9 p.711
Embedded cables, splices	424.40 p.299
Embedded deicing, bridge joints	426.20(E) p.305
Embedded in concrete	360.12(4) p.219
Embedded, Deicing units	426.20(A) p.305
Emergence from the ground	504.80(B) ex. p.397
Emergencies & for tests	590.3(C) p.517
Emergency circuits, boxes	700.10(A) p.623
Emergency illumination, egress lts	700.16 p.626
Emergency lighting circuits	700.15 p.626
Emergency O.C.P., coordination	700.27 I.N. p.627
Emergency systems	Art. 700 p.622
Emergency systems, battery	700.12(A) p.624
Emergency systems, definition	517.2 p.440
Emergency systems, fuel supply	700.12(B2) p.625
Emergency systems, generator	700.12(B) p.625
Emergency systems, loads on b.c.	700.15 p.626
Emergency systems, overcurrent	700.25 p.627
Emergency systems, power 10 sec.	700.12(B5) p.625
Emergency systems, tests	700.3 p.622
Emergency systems, unit equip.	700.12(F) p.625
Emergency systems, wiring	700.10 p.623
Emerging from the ground, cond.	300.5(D1) p.139
EMT raceway, bends	358.26 p.218
EMT raceway, corrosion protected	358.10(B) p.218
EMT raceway, couplings-connectors	358.42 p.219
EMT raceway, maximum size	358.20(B) p.218
EMT raceway, minimum size	358.20(A) p.218
EMT raceway, supports	358.30(B) p.219
EMT, Electrical Metallic Tubing	Art. 358 p.218
EMT, equipment grounding conductor	250.118(4) p.122
EMT, in concrete	358.10(B) p.218
EMT, unbroken lengths	358.30(A) ex.1 p.219
Enamel	358.12(2) p.218
Encapsulated, pool	680.23(B4) p.581
Enclosed overcurrent device	230.208(B) p.88
Enclosed	DEF 100 p.28
Enclosure bonding	250.96 p.118
Enclosure types	110.28 p.39
Enclosures with O.C.P. not as JB	312.8 p.175

Entry	Reference
Enclosures, arcing parts	110.18 p.37
Enclosures, in concrete	314.23(G) p.181
Enclosures, number of circuits	90.8(B) p.24
Enclosures, outer surface	110.12(A) p.33
Enclosures, tunnels, dripproof	110.59 p.44
Enclosures, used as junction box	404.3(B) p.267
End fittings clearance	408.5 p.275
End seal, MI cable	332.40(B) p.195
Enduring the vibration	545.13 p.478
Energized attachments	668.10(A1) p.569
Energized automatically	424.20(A3) p.297
Energized parts	300.31 p.145
Energy reducing maint. switch	240.87 *I.N.* p.98
Enforcement of code	90.4 p.23
Engineering supervision	310.15(C) p.153
ENT	362.1 p.220
ENT, cannot exceed 600v	362.12(5) p.221
ENT, marking	362.120 p.222
ENT, physical damage	362.12(9) p.221
ENT, prewired in concrete slab	300.18(A) p.143
ENT, prewired in concrete slab	362.10(6) p.221
ENT, sizes	362.20 p.221
ENT, strapping	362.30(B) p.222
ENT, through metal studs	300.4(B2) p.136
ENT, wet-niche luminaire	680.23(B) p.580
Entertainment device	522.2DEF p.468
Environmental air duct, plenums	300.22(B) p.144
Environmental conditions, fixture	410.52 p.283
Equal to or greater than	280.4(A) p.132
Equal to or greater than	440.2 p.340
Equalizer leads generators	445.12(E) p.347
Equip. grd. conductor size	T.250.122 p.125
Equip. grd. conductor, earth	250.54 p.113
Equip. over 600v, boiler B.C. require.	490.72(A) p.366
Equip. over 600v, field-fabricated	490.24 p.363
Equip. over 600v, isol switch interlock	490.22 p.363
Equip. over 600v, load interrupters	490.21(E) p.362
Equip. over 600v, oil-filled cutouts	490.21(D) p.362
Equip. over 600v, power fuses	490.21(B1) p.361
Equip. over 600v, switch. conduct.	490.21(E4) p.362
Equip. over 600v, voltage regulators	490.23 p.363
Equipment ground fault time delay	230.95(A) p.87
Equipment grounding cond., EMT	250.118(4) p.122
Equipment grounding means, feeder	215.6 p.60
Equipment likely energized grd.	250.110 p.120
Equipment markings	110.14(C) *I.N.* p.36
Equipment over 600 volts	Art. 490 p.360
Equipment rooms & pits, pools	680.11 p.577
Equipment space, dedicated	110.26(E) p.39
Equipment termination prov.	110.14(C1) p.36
Equipment, communication	90.2(B4) p.22
Equipment, power production	705.2 DEF p.632
Equipotential bond. jumpers	501.125(B) *I.N. #2* p.384
Equipotential plane	682.33 p.592
Equipotential plane, poultry	547.10 p.480
Equivalent strength boxes	314.40(B) ex.1 p.184
Equivalent, to splices	110.14(B) p.36
Equivalent, wall of equipment	110.12(A) p. 35
Escalator, continuous duty	620.61(B2) p.542
Escalators	Art. 620 p.532
Essential b.c. panelboard bonding	517.14 p.443
Essential electrical system	517.30(B1) p.446
Essential electrical system, def.	517.2 p.440
Essential system, transfer switch	517.41(B) p.450
Ethylene	500.6(A3) *I.N.* p.371
Evacuation of a theater	700.12 p.624
Examination of equipment	110.3 p.34
Examples of calculations	pages 804-815
Excavating sidewalks	314.29 p.184
Excess of 2000 amperes	225.30(C) p.74
Exciter, leads	300.3(C2c) p.136
Exciter, overcurrent	445.12 p.347
Exclude moisture	501.15 p.377
Execution of work, workmanlike	800.24 p.670
Exercise of ingenuity	500.5 *I.N. #2* p.399
Exhaust vapors	410.10(C2) p.281
Existing dwelling load additions	220.16 p.63
Exit light, thermal protection	410.130(E3) p.287
Exit lighting emergency systems	700.16 p.626
Exothermic welding	250.64(C) p.114
Exothermic welding process	250.64(C) p.114
Expansion fittings	378.44 p.232
Expansion joints, bonding	250.98 p.118
Expansion joints, raceways	300.7(B) p.140
Expansion, busways	368.244 p.226
Expansion, gutters live parts	366.44 p.223
Expansion, PVC	T.352.44 p.210
Explanatory material FPN	90.5(C) p.24
Explosion proof	DEF 100 p.28
Explosion proof on Class II location	502.5 p.386
Exposed ballasts	410.136(A) p.287
Exposed cable wiring	334.40(B) p.198
Exposed conductive surfaces,	DEF 517.2 p.441
Exposed current to bodies	517.64(A) p.455
Exposed non-curr. carry parts	250.114 p.121
Expulsion type fuse links	490.21(C) p.362
Extension cord listing	240.5(B4) p.91
Extension cord sets	590.6(B2) p.518
Extension rings	314.16(A) p.178
Extension through walls	376.10(4) p.230
Extensions, branch circuit	210.12(B) p.52
Extensions from box	314.22 p.180
Extensions from wireways	376.70 p.231
Extensions, underplaster	382.30 p.234

Extensive metal on buildings	250.116 **I.N.** p.122	FCC, insulating ends	324.40(A) p.189
External means for adjusting	240.6(B) p.91	FCC, marking	324.120(A) p.190
External sensing elements	430.225(B1) p.334	FCC, metal components	324.101 p.190
External joiners, raceway	T.384.22 * note p. 236	FCC, polarization	324.40(B) p.190
External spark, batteries	480.10(A) p.360	FCC, receptacle	324.42 (A&B) p.190
Extra-hard usage cords arc lamps	520.61 p.466	FCC, release-type adhesive	324.41 p.190
Extra-hard usage cords type	520.68(A) p.467	FCC, shields	324.40(C) p.190
Extra-hard usage cords, ampacity	T.520.44 p.463	FCC, system height	324.10(G) p.189
Extra-hard usage, Class I	501.10(B2) p.377	FCC, transition assembly	324.40(D) p.190
Extreme cold	378.10(3) **I.N.** p.231	FCC, voltage 300v	324.10(B1) p.189
Extreme cold	352.10 **I.N.** p.208	Feeder tap, 10 feet	240.21(B1) p.92
Extruded thermoplastic covering	382.2 p.233	Feeder tap, not over 25 feet	240.21(B2) p.93
		Feeder tap, over 25' to 100'	240.21(B3&4) p.93
		Feeder taps, motors	430.28 p.318
-F-		Feeder, ampacity minimum	215.2(A1) p.59
		Feeder, com. neutral same raceway	215.4(B) p.60
Face up position receptacles	406.5(E) p.272	Feeder, common neutral	215.4(A) p.60
Faceplate thickness, switches	404.9(C) p.268	Feeder, demand fact. elevators	T.620.14 p.536
Faceplate, boxes	314.25 p.182	Feeder, diagram	215.5 p. 60
Faceplates, metal, grounded	406.6(B) p.272	Feeder, equip. grounding means	215.6 p.60
Faceplates, receptacles	406.5 p.271	Feeder, GFCI equipment	215.10 p.60
Faceplates, thickness	406.5(A) p.271	Feeder, GFCI personnel	215.9 p.60
Facilitate cleaning hood fixture	410.10(C3) p.281	Feeder, minimum size	215.2(A) p.59
Facilitate overcurrent device	250.4(B4) p.103	Feeder, mobile homes	550.31 p.489
Facilitate removal or disconnection	422.16(A) p.292	Feeder, over 600v O.C.P.	240.100 p.100
Factory assembled, NMC	334.2 p.196	Feeder, permanently installed	550.10(A) p.482
Factory-applied shield, stress reduct.	300.40 p.146	Feeder, supplied by other structure	225.30 p.74
Factory-installed internal wiring	90.7 p.24	Feeder, tapped two-wire circuits	215.7 p.60
Fair, GFCI receptacles	525.23(A1) p.471	Feeders, floating buildings	553.6 p.512
Fair, multiple services	525.11 p.470	Feeders, motors	430.24 p.318
Falling dirt, motor enclosure	T.110.28 p.41	Feeders, shore power	555.19(A3) p.515
Fan circuit interlock	424.63 p.300	Feeders, studios 400%	530.18(B) p.474
Fans, ceiling support 35 pounds	422.18 p.293	Feeders, X-ray	660.6(B) p.566
Fans, paddle outlet box	314.27(D) p.183	Female fitting, showcase	410.59(C3) p.284
Far away as possible, vent trans.	450.45(A) p.355	Fence	110.31 p.40
Farm buildings conductors	220.103 p.70	Fence fabric	110.31 p.40
Farm loads	220.103 p.70	Fence to live parts, distance	T.110.31 p.40
Fastening unbroken lengths EMT	358.30(A) ex.1 p.219	Ferromagnetic envelope definition	426.2 p.304
Fault closing rating, feeder	225.52(B) p.76	Ferromagnetic, single conductor	427.47 p. 309
Fault hazard current	517.160(B) p.457	Ferrous enclosures	300.20(A ex 2) p.144
Fault hazard current, definition	517.2 p.441	Ferrous metal conduit, corrosion	344.10(B) p.204
FC assemblies tap devices	322.10 p.188	Ferrous metal, faceplates	406.6(A) p.272
FC cable definition	322.2 p.188	Ferrous raceways corrosion prot.	300.6(A) p.139
FC cable, taps	322.56(B) p.188	Festoon lighting	225.6(B) p.71
FC cable, terminal block ident.	322.120(C) p.188	Festoon supports	225.6(B) p.71
FCC system, crossings	324.18 p.189	Festoon wiring, fixtures	410.54(A) p.283
FCC, cable connections	324.40(A) p.189	Festoon wiring, staggered	520.65 p.467
FCC, carpet squares	324.1 p.189	Festoons, stage	520.65 p.467
FCC, construction	324.100 p.190	Flexible connect., Class II, Div.1	502.10(2) p.386
FCC, corrosion-resistance	324.101 p.190	Fiberboard, cellulose low-density	410.136(B) p.288
FCC, crossings	324.18 p.189	Fiber to the premises, FTTP	840.2 DEF p.707
FCC, definition	324.2 p.189	Fibers Class III location	503.1 p.391

Entry	Reference
Field marking, available fault current	110.24(A) p.37
Field punched metal studs	300.4(B1) p.136
Field-wiring chamber	680.23(F1) p.581
Film & film scrap	530.41 p.475
Film or tape	530.1 p.472
Final conductor span	225.19 ex.4 p.73
Fine print note (FPN)	90.5(C) p.24
Finished ceilings, paint, wallpaper	424.42 p. 299
Fire alarm circuit integrity, CI	760.176(G) p.658
Fire alarm circuit integrity, CI DEF	760.2 p.651
Fire alarm systems	760.1 I.N. #1 p.651
Fire alarm, supply side	230.94 ex.4 p.86
Fire barriers, busway	368.234 p.226
Fire circuits, conductors	760.49 p.653
Fire circuits, diff. cir. same cable	760.48 p.653
Fire circuits, overcurrent	760.43 p.652
Fire circuits, power limitations	760.121 p.654
Fire circuits, wiring methods	760.53(A) p.654
Fire detectors	760.145 p.657
Fire escape, conductors	225.6(B) p.71
Fire escapes, vent transformer	450.45(A) p.355
Fire point, transformer liquid	450.24 p.353
Fire prot., water pump remote disc	230.72(A) ex p.85
Fire protection, transformer vault	450.47 p.355
Fire protective signaling systems	Art. 760 p.651
Fire protective signaling	760.136(A) p.656
Fire pump circuit	240.4(A) p.89
Fire pump, service conductors	695.3(A1) p.616
Fire pump, supply conductors	695.6(A&B) p.618
Fire pump, supply side	230.94 ex.4 p.86
Fire pump, voltage drop	695.7 p.620
Fire pumps	695.6(H) p.619
Fire pumps, disconnects	230.72(A) ex. p.85
Fire pumps, separate service	230.2(A1) p.78
Fire resistance CATV cables	820.179(C) p.695
Fire resistance comm. wire	800.179(I) I.N. p.681
Fire resistive ratings	300.21 I.N. p.144
Fire retardant fibrous covering	320.104 p.187
Fire stop, all holes	300.21 p.144
Fire/smoke dampers	645.4(2) p.560
Fireplaces, wall space	210.52(A2) p.56
Fire-rated floor	300.11(A1) p.141
Fire-resistant, low smoke	300.22(C3) p.145
First-make, last-break plug	250.124(A) p.124
Fish the cables	300.4(D) ex.2 p.137
Fished in wall, NM box	334.30(B1) p.197
Fittings design. for the purp.	400.10 I.N. p.260
Fittings, aluminum to steel tube	358.12 ex. p.218
Fittings, insulated	300.4(G) p.137
Fittings, support 50 pounds	314.27(A2) p.183
Fittings, where required	300.15 p.142
Five threads fully engaged	500.8(E1) p.375
Fixed appliance, definition	550.2 p.481
Fixed appliances, feeder load 75%	220.53 p.65
Fixed grounding poles	406.10 p.273
Fixed ladders, corrosion resistant	314.72(A) p.186
Fixed wiring substitute, cords as	400.8(1) p.260
Fixture as raceways	410.64 p.285
Fixture canopy, box cover	410.22 p.282
Fixture chains, stranded conduct.	410.56(E) p.284
Fixture exposed within hood	410.10(C3) p.281
Fixture hangers, flat cable	322.40(B) p.188
Fixture load current	410.62(C3) p.284
Fixture stems, arms or stems	410.56(C) p.284
Fixture stems, splices and taps	410.56(D) p.284
Fixture studs, boxes	314.16(B3) p.178
Fixture studs, not part of box	410.36(C) p.283
Fixture wire SF-1 voltage	T.402.3 p.262
Fixture wire, ampacity	402.5 p.262
Fixture wires	Art. 402 p.262
Fixture wires, marking	402.9(A&B) p.266
Fixture wires, minimum size	402.6 p.266
Fixture wires, protection	240.4 p.89
Fixture wires, uses permitted	402.10 p.266
Fixture, adjacent comb. material	410.118 p.286
Fixture, adjustable	410.62(B) p.284
Fixture, autotransformer	410.138 p.288
Fixture, ballast install fiberboard	410.136(B) p.288
Fixture, ballast marking	410.74(A) p.285
Fixture, clothes closet	410.16(C) p.281
Fixture, combustible material	410.115(A) p.286
Fixture, combustible shades	410.70 p.285
Fixture, conductor insulation	410.52 p.283
Fixture, conductor size	410.52 p.283
Fixture, considered as alive	410.140(C) p.288
Fixture, construction	410.118 p.286
Fixture, crowfeet	410.36(C) p.283
Fixture, DC current	410.134 p.287
Fixture, dimension	410.30(A) p.282
Fixture, disconnection	410.141(A) p.288
Fixture, electrical rating	410.74(B) p.285
Fixture, electric-discharge	410.140(A) p.288
Fixture, end-to-end assembly	410.64(C) p.285
Fixture, exposed ballasts	410.136(A) p.287
Fixture, exposed metal parts	410.46 p.283
Fixture, fastened to ceiling	410.36(B) p.282
Fixture, fire resistant material	410.115(B) p.286
Fixture, flush & recessed	410.110 p.286
Fixture, glass lamps	410.42 p.283
Fixture, handhole	410.30(B) p.282
Fixture, heavy-duty track	410.153 p.289
Fixture, hickeys	410.36(C) p.283
Fixture, high-intensity discharge	410.130(F) p.287
Fixture, insulating joints	410.36(D) p.283

Entry	Reference	Page
Fixture, lamp replacement	410.142	p.288
Fixture, lamp wattage marking	410.120	p.286
Fixture, lens pool 18"	680.23(A5)	p.580
Fixture, movable or flexible parts	410.56(E)	p.284
Fixture, polarization	410.50	p.283
Fixture, recessed clearance	410.116(A)	p.286
Fixture, recessed fluorescent	410.16(A2)	p.281
Fixture, recessed incandescent	410.16(A1)	p.281
Fixture, screw-shell max. weight	410.30(A)	p.282
Fixture, stranded conductors	410.56(E)	p.284
Fixture, supports	410.30(A)	p.282
Fixture, surface-mounted	410.16(A1)	p.281
Fixture, tap conductors	410.117(C)	p.286
Fixture, temperature	410.118	p.286
Fixture, tension	410.56(F)	p.284
Fixture, thermal insulation	410.116(B)	p.286
Fixture, track conductors	410.155(A)	p.289
Fixture, track fastening	410.154	p.289
Fixture, tree mounting	410.36(G)	p.283
Fixture, tripods	410.36(C)	p.283
Fixture, weight 50 pounds	314.27(A1)	p.182
Fixture, weight 6 pounds	410.30(A)	p.282
Fixture, whip flex. conduit	250.118(7b)	p.123
Fixtures, aiming or adjusting	410.62(B)	p.284
Fixtures, in clothes closets	410.16	p.281
Fixtures, in ducts or hoods	410.10(C)	p.281
Fixtures, in show windows	410.14	p.281
Fixtures, inspection of	410.8	p.280
Fixtures, near combust. material	410.11	p.281
Fixtures, no-niche	680.23(D)	p.581
Fixtures, over bathtub	410.10(D)	p.281
Fixtures, over combust. material	410.12	p.281
Fixtures, over vehicle lanes	511.7(B1b)	p.421
Fixtures, suspended ceilings	410.36(B)	p.282
Fixtures, temperature 90° C	410.11	p.281
Fixtures, wet locations	410.10(A)	p.281
Fixtures, wet-niche	680.23(B1)	p.580
Flame arrestor, batteries	480.10(A)	p.360
Flame-retardant covering	340.116	p.202
Flame-retardant jacket	336.116	p.200
Flame-retardant NMC cable	334.116(B)	p.198
Flame-retardant, hoistway wiring	620.11(A)	p.534
Flammable anesthetics stored	517.60(A2)	p.453
Flammable anesthetics, definition	517.2	p.441
Flammable disinfecting agents	517.60(A2)	p.453
Flammable gases or vapors	500.5(A)	p.399
Flammable oil	490.3	p.360
Flammable paints are dried	516.3(E)	p.436
Flammable paints dried	516.3(F)	p.436
Flanged surface inlet, fixtures	410.62(C3)	p.284
Flanged surface inlets, stage	520.53(M)	p.466
Flash point, transformer	450.24	p.353
Flash protection, markings	110.16	p.37
Flashers, cutouts	600.6(B)	p.520
Flashers, switches	600.6(B)	p.520
Flat cable assemblies, protection	322.100	p.188
Flat cable assemblies, term. block	322.120(C)	p.188
Flat cable assemblies, uses permitted	322.10	p.188
Flat conductor cable	324.1	p.189
Flatirons, temperature limiting	422.46	p.294
Flat-top raceways	390.3(A)	p.238
Flex. cords & cables protection	400.14	p.260
Flex. metal cond., equip. grd.	250.118(5)a	p.122
Flex. metal cond., number of cond.	T.348.22	p.206
Flex. metal conduit, interconnect.	410.137(C)	p.288
Flexible cord pendants	314.25(C)	p.182
Flexible cords and cables	Art. 400	p.251
Flexible cords, grounded conductor	400.22	p.261
Flexible cords, physical damage	620.21(A2c)	p.537
Flexible cords, protection	240.5	p.90
Flexible cords, ranges & dryers	T.400.4	p.251
Flexible metal conduit	Art. 350	p.207
Flexible metal conduit, supports	348.30	p.206
Flexible metallic tubing	360.1	p.219
Flexible metallic tubing, min. size	360.20(A)	p.219
Flexural capability	426.21(D)	p.305
Floating buildings	90.2(A1)	p.22
Floating buildings, wiring meth.	553.7(B)	p.512
Floating dock, service location	555.7	p.513
Floating piers	555.2(3)	p.513
Floating restaurant	90.2(A1)	p.22
Floodplain protection	708.10(C3)	p.638
Floor boxes	250.146(C)	p.127
Floor boxes	314.27(B)	p.183
Floor boxes 18" to wall	210.52(A3)	p.56
Floor covering, under heat panels	424.99(B)	p.304
Floor or working platform, switch	404.8(A)	p.267
Floor receptacle	210.52(A3)	p.56
Floor receptacles, protection	406.9(D)	p.273
Floor to structural ceiling	408.18	p.275
Flourescent fixture, fastened T-Bars	410.36(B)	p.282
Fluidized beds, spray area	516.10(C4)	p.439
Fluor. exit fixt., therm. protect.	410.130(E2)	p.287
Fluor. fixture, egress lighting	410.130(E4)	p.287
Fluor. light fixtures, independent	410.24(A)	p.282
Fluorescent fixt., as raceway	410.64	p.285
Fluorescent fixt., thermal protect.	410.130(E)	p.287
Fluoroscopic, X-ray	660.23(A)	p.566
Flush lights, clearance	410.116	p.286
Flush lights, temperature limit	410.115(A)	p.286
Flush mount recept. faceplate	406.9(E)	p.273
Flying material, motors	430.16	p.316
Flying	506.2	p.412
Flyings, Class III	503.1	p.391

FMT size	360.20(B) p.219	Furnace, individual branch circuit	422.12 p.292
Foot switches, induction heat	665.7(B) p.567	Furniture, permanent	210.60(B) p.58
Footlights, stage	520.43 p.462	Fuse links, expulsion type	490.21(C) p.362
Foreign systems, condensation	110.26(E1b) p.39	Fuse, controlled vented power	DEF 100 p.34
Foreign systems, protection from	110.26(E1b) p.39	Fuse, Edison-base type	240.51(B) p.96
Formal interpretations of the Code	90.6 p.24	Fuse, electronically actuated	DEF 100 p.33
Forming shell, definition	680.2 p.575	Fuse, marking	240.50(B) p.96
Forming shell, pool	680.23(B1) p.580	Fuse, maximum voltage	240.50(A) p.96
Fountain, bonding	680.53 p.588	Fuse, vented power	DEF 100 p.34
Fountain, cord length	680.51(E) p.588	Fused switches	404.17 p.270
Fountain, DEF	680.2 p.576	Fuseholders	240.60 p.97
Fountain, GFCI	680.51(A) p.588	Fuseholders, deenergized	490.21(B6) p.361
Fountain, grounding	680.54 p.588	Fuseless protectors	800.90(A1) p.672
Fountain, pumps	680.51(B) p.588	Fuses or breakers in parallel	240.8 p.91
Fountains	680.50 p.588	Fuses that expel flame	490.21(B5) p.361
Fountains, signs	680.57 p.589	Fuses, adapters	240.54 p.96
Foyers not part of hallway	210.52(I) p.58	Fuses, cartridge	240.60 p.97
FPL cable	760.179(F) p.659	Fuses, disconnecting means	240.40 p.96
FPLP cable	760.179(D) p.659	Fuses, in clothes closets	240.24(D) p.95
FPLR cable	760.179(E) p.659	Fuses, next higher size	240.4(B) p.90
Fractions of ampere	220.5(B) p.61	Fuses, next higher size motor	430.52(C1) ex.1 p.322
Fractions of ampere, D example	p.804	Fuses, parallel	240.8 p.91
Frame of a vehicle, grounding	250.34(B) p.110	Fuses, plug	240.50 p.96
Frames of ranges & dryers	250.140 p.126	Fuses, readily accessible	240.24(A) p.95
Frames of stationary motors	430.242 p.335	Fuses, standard sizes	240.6 p.91
Framing member, cable support	300.4(D) p.137	Fuses, Type S	240.53(A) p.96
Framing members, as support	314.23(D) p.180	Fusible link cable connector	450.6(A3) p.351
Free air, conductors	T.310.15(B)(17) p.155	Fusion apparatus, spray area	516.3(F) p.436
Free circulation of air	110.13(B) p.35	Future expansion and convenience	90.8(A) p. 24
Free conductor at box, length 6"	300.14 p.142		
Free from short circuits	110.7 p.35		
Free nonheating leads	424.43(A) p.299	-G-	
Free standing partitions, outlets	605.8 p.527		
Freedom from hazard	90.1(B) p.22		
Freezing of piping	422.50 p.295	G or GR green or ground	250.126(3) p.125
Freight station circuits	110.19 ex. p.37	G.F.P. of heat tracing	427.22 p.308
Freight station	110.19 ex. p.37	G.F.P. of heating panels	427.22 p.308
Frequencies of 360hz and higher	310.10 ex.1 p.149	Gallery, live parts	430.231 p.335
Frost heaves or settlement	300.5(J) *I.N.* p.139	Galvanic action, EMT	358.12(6) p.218
FTTP (fiber to the premises)	840.2 Def. p.707	Galvanic action, IMC conduit	342.14 p.202
Fuel cell system	Art. 692 p.607	Galvanic action, rigid conduit	344.14 p.204
Fuel cell, definition	692.2 p.607	Gantry, overhead	626.23 p.549
Fuel shut-off	692.54 p.609	Garage	DEF 100 p.28
Fuel supply, emerg. systems	700.12(B2) p.625	Garage, detached	210.52(G1) p.58
Fuel tanks, aircraft	513.3(C) p.422	Garages snap switch disconnect	225.36 ex. p.75
Full-load current 1 ø motors	T.430.248 p.337	Garages, above floor level 18"	511.3(D1B) p.420
Full-load current 2 ø motors	T.430.249 p.337	Garages, commercial	Art. 511 p.419
Full-load current 3 ø motors	T.430.250 p.338	Garages, parking	511.3(A) p.420
Full-load current D.C. motors	T.430.247 p.336	Garages, pit or depression	511.3(C3B) p.420
Fumes, exposed to	110.11 p.35	Garages, portable light	511.4(B2) p.421
Fungus-resistant NMC cable	334.116(B) p.198	Garages, residential GFCI	210.8(A2) p.50
Furnace transformer	450.26 ex.3 p.353	Garages, residential receptacles	210.52(G) p.58

Garbage disposal, cord length	422.16(B1) p.292
Gas discharge from interrupt. devices	490.39 p.364
Gas fired range receptacles	210.52(B2) ex.2 p.56
Gas furnace, branch circuit	422.12 p.292
Gas pipe, bonding	250.104(B) p.119
Gas pipe, grounding electrode	250.52(B) p.112
Gas pipe, in raceways	300.8 p.140
Gas piping, bonding jumper	250.104(B) p.119
Gas pressure, IGS cable 20 pounds	326.112 p.191
Gas range, mobile home	550.16(B3) p.487
Gas range, small appliance circuit	210.52(B2)ex.2 p.56
Gas spacer cable, ampacity	T.326.80 p.191
Gas station, double-pole switch	514.11(A) p.428
Gas tubing support, signs	600.41(B) p.524
Gas, protective	506.2 p. 412
Gases, exposed to	110.11 p.35
Gasketed busways	501.10(B1)(3) p.376
Gasketed wireways	501.10(B1)(3) p.376
Gasketed-type fixtures in ducts	300.22(B) p.144
Gasoline dispensing stations	Art. 514 p.425
General care area receptacles	517.18(B) p.444
General lighting loads	T.220.12 p.63
General lighting, demand factors	T.220.42 p.64
General-purpose enclosures	501.115(B2) p.383
Generator, ampacity	445.13 p.347
Generator, balancer sets	445.12(D) p.347
Generator, field control	620.13 I.N. p.535
Generator, less than 65 volts	445.12(C) p.347
Generator, output	665.5 p.567
Generator, standby system	701.10 p.628
Generator, vehicle mounted	250.34(B) p.110
GFCI, accessory building	210.8(A2) p.50
GFCI, apartment outdoors	210.8(B4) p.51
GFCI, auto diagnostic equip.	511.12 p.422
GFCI, basements	210.8(A5) p.50
GFCI, boathouses	210.8(A8) p.50
GFCI, carnivals	525.23 p.471
GFCI, commercial bathrooms	210.8(B1) p.51
GFCI, commercial garages	511.12 p.422
GFCI, construction sites	590.6 p.518
GFCI, counter top surfaces	210.8(A6) p.50
GFCI, crawl spaces	210.8(A4) p.50
GFCI, datum plane	682.15 p. 592
GFCI, dwelling units	210.8(A) p.50
GFCI, electrically heated floors	424.44(G) p.300
GFCI, elevators	620.85 p.543
GFCI, Fairs, Carnivals	525.23(A1) p.471
GFCI, fountain	680.51(A) p.588
GFCI, fully selective health care	517.17(C) p.443
GFCI, garages dwelling	210.8(A2) p.50
GFCI, industrial bathrooms	210.8(B1) p. 51
GFCI, kitchen countertop	210.8(A6) p.50
GFCI, kitchen sink	210.8(A7) p.50
GFCI, luminaire hydromassage room	680.72 p.590
GFCI, marinas	210.8(A8) p.50
GFCI, mobile homes	550.13(B) p.484
GFCI, outdoor portable sign	600.10(C2) p.522
GFCI, outdoors dwelling	210.8(A3) p. 50
GFCI, performance testing	230.95(C) p.87
GFCI, pool light low volt-contact	680.23(A3) p.580
GFCI, pools	680.5 p.577
GFCI, pools storable	680.32 p.585
GFCI, portable sign	600.10(C2) p.522
GFCI, receptacles on roofs	210.8(B3) p.51
GFCI, replacement receptacles	406.4(D3) p.271
GFCI, service disconnect	230.95 ex.1 p.87
GFCI, service setting	230.95(A) p.87
GFCI, solidly grounded wye	230.95 p.87
GFCI, spa/hot tub	680.43(A2) p.587
GFCI, spas and hot tubs	680.44(C) p.587
GFCI, temporary wiring	590.6(A) p.518
GFCI, unfinished basements	210.8(A5) p.50
GFCI, vending machines	422.51 p. 295
GFCI, wet bar sink 6 feet	210.8(A7) p.50
GFCI, will afford no protection	230.95(C) *I.N.#1* p.87
Glass knobs, open conductors	225.12 p.72
Glass lamps, fixtures	410.42 p.283
Glue houses, corrosive prot.	300.6(D) *I.N.* p.140
Gongs	620.2 p.533
Gooseneck, services	230.54(B) p.83
Governmental authority	708.1 *I.N. #1* p.636
Governmental bodies	90.4 p.23
Grade level access 6' 6"	210.52(E1) p.57
Grain drying systems	T.220.103 note p.70
Gratings, vault door	450.45(C) p.355
Gravel	314.29 ex. p.184
Gray, color	200.7(C2) p.47
Grd. circuit conductor, appliances	200.10(E) p.48
Grd. elect. cond., metal enclosures	250.64(E) p.114
Grd. electrode cond. protection	250.64(B) p.114
Grd. liquidtight flex metal	250.118(B&D) p.122
Grd., concrete, brick, tile	T.110.26(A1) cond 1 p.38
Grease, oil or cooking vapors	410.10(C2) p.281
Green-colored conductor	250.119 p.123
Green-colored hex headed screw	406.9(B1) p.273
Green-colored rigid ear adapter	406.9(B3) p.273
Greenfield conduit	Art. 348 p.205
Grommets, metal studs	300.4(B1) p.136
Ground as grounding	250.142(A) p.126
Ground clamps	250.70 p.116
Ground clamps, connection	250.70 p.116
Ground clamps, protection	250.10 p.103
Ground current detection 600v	490.72(D) p.366
Ground detectors	250.21(B) p.104

Ground fault equipment time delay	230.95(A) p.87
Ground fault protect. service	230.95 ex.1 p.87
Ground fault protection test on site	230.95(C) p.87
Ground fault tripping bands	708.52(D) p.640
Ground movement	300.5(J) p.139
Ground return, trolley wires	110.19 p.37
Ground ring depth 2 1/2'	250.53(F) p.113
Ground rod accessible	250.68(A) p.115
Ground rod connection	250.70 p.116
Ground rod driven depth	250.53(G) p.113
Ground rod in soil 8'	250.53(G) p.113
Ground rod resistance 25 ohm	250.52(A2) ex p.112
Ground rod size	250.52(A5) p.112
Ground rod, #6 wire size	250.66(A) p.115
Grounded cond. disc. simult.	404.2(B) ex.1 p.266
Grounded cond., change in size	240.23 p.95
Grounded conductor	210.6(C2) p.50
Grounded conductor flexible cord	400.22(B) p.261
Grounded conductor, 3 white stripes	200.6(A) p.46
Grounded conductor, 50v or less	200.7(B) p.47
Grounded conductor, clearly evident	200.10(A) p.47
Grounded conductor, identification	200.6 p.46
Grounded conductor, insulated	200.2 p.46
Grounded metal barrier	680.23(2) p.580
Grounded shield, transformer	426.31 p.306
Grounded, clothes dryer	250.140 p.126
Grounded, electrically continuous	250.52(A1) p.111
Grounded, metal faceplates	406.6(B) p.272
Grounded, ranges	250.140 p.126
Grounded, service cond. min. size	250.24(C) p.105
Grounding cond., communication	800.100(A3) p.673
Grounding conductor aluminum	250.64(A) p.113
Grounding conductor connections	250.70 p.116
Grounding conductor, coaxial	820.100(A3) p.689
Grounding conductor, sizing	T.250.122 p.125
Grounding connections	250.24(A) p.104
Grounding elect. cond. connection	250.24(D) p.105
Grounding elect. cond. connection	250.68(B) p.116
Grounding elect. cond. joint/ splice	250.64(C) p.114
Grounding elect. cond. protection	250.64(B) p.114
Grounding electrode 25 ohms	250.52(A2) p.112
Grounding electrode bare #4 20'	250.52(A3) p.112
Grounding electrode bonding	250.60 *I.N. #2* p.113
Grounding electrode conductor size	250.66 p.115
Grounding electrode in soil 8'	250.53(G) p.113
Grounding electrode system	250.50 p.111
Grounding electrode, min. size	250.52(A5a) p.112
Grounding electrodes mult.	250.52 p.111
Grounding electrodes, bonded together	250.50 p.111
Grounding or bond. cond. derating	310.15(B6) p.152
Grounding poles, fixed	406.10(A) p.273
Grounding sheath or braid	426.27 p.306
Grounding, bridge frame	610.61 p.532
Grounding, deep well pumps	250.112(L) p.121
Grounding, metal elbow	250.86 ex. 3 p.117
Grounding, motor control center	430.96 p.329
Grounding, pool equipment	680.6 p.577
Grounding, surface metal raceway	386.60 p.237
Grounding, trolley frame	610.61 p.532
Grounding-pole identification	406.10(B) p.273
Group-operated switches 600v	460.24(A) p.358
Guard strips, cable protection	320.23(B) p.186
Guarded	DEF 100 p.29
Guards, portable handlamps	410.82(B) p.285
Guest room	DEF 100 p.29
Guest room, permanent cooking	210.18 p.52
Guest rooms, receptacle placement	210.60(B) p.58
Guest rooms, receptacles	210.60(B) p.58
Guest rooms, suites	210.18 p. 52
Guest suite	DEF 100 p.29
Gutters, bare live parts	366.100(E) p.224
Gutters, busbar ampacity	366.23(A) p.223
Gutters, construction	366.100 p.224
Gutters, extend beyond equip. 30'	366.12(2) p.223
Gutters, number of conductors 30	366.22(A) p.223
Gutters, splices and taps 75%	366.56(A) p.223
Gutters, support	366.30(B) p.223
Guys or braces, service mast	230.28 p.80

-H-

Habitable rooms	210.8(A5) p.50
Hair dryer, cord protection	422.41 p.294
Half-round raceways	390.4(A) p.238
Hallway, foyer not part of	210.52(I) p.58
Hallway, receptacle 10'	210.52(H) p.58
Halon sprinklers	450.43(A) ex. p.354
Hand gun, sprayer	516.10(B2) ex. p.439
Hand-held tools, grounding	250.114(ex.) p.121
Handhole for metal pole	410.30(B) p. 282
Handlamps, construction	410.82(B) p.285
Handle ties	240.15(B1) p.92
Handle ties, breakers	230.71(B) p.84
Handle ties, single pole breakers	240.15(B4) p.92
Handle, switch operating height	404.8(A) p.267
Handles or levers, breakers	240.41(B) p.96
Hangars, aircraft definition	513.2 p.422
Hard or soft conversion, definition	90.9 *I.N.* p.25
Hard service cord, splices	400.9 p.260
Hard service cords	T.400.4 p.251
Hard-rubber bushing	314.25(C) p.182
Hard-service type cord	410.59(A) p.284

Entry	Reference
Hard-usage, cords for fixtures	410.62(B) p.284
Harmonic currents, busways	368.258 p.226
Harmonic currents, cords	400.5 p.258
Harmonic neutral currents	210.4(A) *I.N.* p.48
Harmonic neutral currents	220.61(C) p.67
Harmonic neutral currents	310.15(B5)(C) p.152
Hazard current, definition	517.2 p.441
Hazard, free from	90.1(B) p.22
Hazard, power loss O.C.P.	240.4(A) p.89
Hazardous area documented	500.4(A) p.368
Hazardous location, cables	725.3(D) p.641
Hazardous locations	Art. 500 p.367
Hazardous, temp. ID numbers	T.500.8(C) p.374
HDPE conduit, size	353.20(B) p.211
Header, definition	372.2 p.228
Header, definition	374.2 p.229
Headroom, equipment 6 1/2'	110.26(A3) p.38
Health care facilities, definition	Art. 517 p.440
Health care facility GFCI	517.17(B) p.443
Health care facility, grd. fault prot.	517.17(A) p.443
Health care low volt. bodies 10v	517.64(A1) p.455
Health Care, nonmetallic conduit	517.30(C3)(2) p.447
Heart muscle	517.11 *I.N.* p.443
Heat tape outlet	550.13(E) p.485
Heat, branch circuit rating	424.3(A) p.296
Heat, dissipation of conductors	300.17 p.142
Heated appliance signal	422.42 p.294
Heated appliances, cord 50w	422.43(A) p.294
Heated ceilings, wiring clearance	424.36 p.298
Heater cord	T.400.4 p.252
Heater, air flow	424.59 p.300
Heater, cords over 50 watt	422.43(A) p.294
Heater, disconnect	424.19 p.296
Heater, unit switch marked off	424.19(C) p.297
Heaters 50kw or more, subdivided	424.22(E) p.298
Heaters rated 50kw or more, B.C.	424.22(D) p.298
Heaters, duct work	424.12(B) p.296
Heaters, electrical components	424.12(B) p.296
Heaters, pool	680.9 p.577
Heaters, wired sections	424.12(B) p.296
Heating assemblies, disconnect	427.55(B) p.310
Heating blankets	427.2 *I.N.* p.307
Heating cable	427.2 *I.N.* p.307
Heating cable, inspection & tests	424.45 p.300
Heating cables, concrete 16 1/2w	424.44(A) p.299
Heating cables, adjacent runs	424.41(B) p.299
Heating cables, ceiling surface	424.41(E) p.299
Heating cables, construction	424.34 p.298
Heating cables, crossing joists	424.41(J) p.299
Heating cables, dryboard	424.41 p.299
Heating cables, gypsum board	424.41(C) p.299
Heating cables, in plaster	424.41 p.299
Heating cables, joists	424.41(I) p.299
Heating cables, lead wires	424.35 p.298
Heating cables, length 7' leads	424.34 p.298
Heating cables, marking	424.35 p.298
Heating cables, paint	424.42 p.299
Heating cables, secured 16"	424.41(F) p.299
Heating cables, splices	424.41(D) p.299
Heating cables, voltage colors	424.35 p.298
Heating cables, wallpaper	424.42 p.299
Heating elements, cable separation	424.39 p.299
Heating elements, marking appl.	422.61 p.295
Heating elements, marking heat	424.29 p.298
Heating elements, resistance	422.11(F) p.291
Heating elements, resistance	424.22(B) p.297
Heating elements, subdivided	422.11(F) p.291
Heating equipment branch cts.	424.3(A) p.296
Heating equipment, frequency	665.27 p.568
Heating panel set	424.91 p.302
Heating panel set, nailing	424.93(B3) p.303
Heating panels, from boxes 8"	424.39 p.299
Heating panels, in concrete 33w	424.98(A) p.303
Heating panels, radiant	424.90 p.302
Heating panels, under floor cover	424.99(B) p.304
Heating tape	427.2 *I.N.* p.307
Heating, disconnect	424.19 p.296
Heating, impedance	426.30 p.306
Heating, induction	427.36 p.309
Heating, induction-dielectric	Art. 665 p.567
Heating, pipelines & vessels	Art. 427 p.307
Heating, skin effect	426.40 p.306
Heavy-capacity feeders	430.62(B) p.325
Heavy-duty lampholder 600va	220.14(E) p.62
Heavy-duty lampholder sockets	210.21(A) p.54
Heavy-duty track, fixtures	410.153 p.289
Held in free air, opposite polarity	T.408.56 p.277
Hermetic comp. disconnect	440.12(A) p.342
Hermetic comp. hp disconnect	440.6(A) ex.1 p.341
Hermetic refrigerant motor-comp.	440.2 p.340
Hexafluoride gas	326.112 p.191
Hexagonal headed screw, green	406.10(B1) p.273
Hexagonal shape, fuse	240.50(C) p.96
Hickeys, boxes	314.16(B3) p.178
Hickeys, fixtures	410.36(C) p.283
HID circuit breakers	240.83(D) p.97
High bay manufact. bldg.	240.21(B4) p.93
High volt. power dist., tunnels	110.51(A) p.43
High voltage	DEF 490.2 p.360
High voltage conductors, tunnels	110.53 p.44
Highest locked-rotor, motors	430.7(B) 3 p.313
Highest water level mark	626.22(B) p.549
High-impedance grd. neutral	250.20(D) p.104
High-impedance grd. neutral	250.36(B) p.111

High-impedance shunts	230.94 ex. 2 p.86	Hypobaric facilities	517.34(B4) p.449
High-intensity discharge fixtures	410.130(F) p.287	Hysteresis	300.20(B) *I.N.* p.144
High-leg, feeder orange color	110.15 p.36		
High-pressure spray machines	422.49 p. 295		
High-voltage definition	490.2 p.360	\-I-	
High-voltage fuses	490.21(B) p.361		
High-voltage grids spray appl.	516.10(A1) ex.p.438		
High-voltage in concrete	T.300.50 p.146	Identification of conductors	Article 200 p.46
Hi-intensity discharge fixtures	410.130(F) p.287	Identification of disconnect	110.22 p.37
Hinged or held captive, lamps	410.142 p.288	Identification of terminals	200.10(B) p.48
Hinged panels or doors 90°	110.26(A2) p.38	Ignition systems receptacle	210.52(B2) ex.2 p.56
Hoist, protected by fuse & C.B.	610.42(A) p.531	Ignitible concentrations	500.5(B2)(2) p.370
Hoists & cranes	Art. 610 p.527	Ignitible fiber	506.5 p. 414
Hoists, boat	210.8(C) p. 51	Ignitible flammable gases & vapors	500.7(K2) p.373
Hoists, monorail supports	610.21(C) p.530	Ignitible material, closets	240.24(D) p.95
Hoistway door interlock wiring	620.11(A) p.534	Igniting the flammable gas	DEF 500 p.367
Hoistway pit access door	620.24(B) p.538	Ignition of gases, batteries	480.9(A) p.360
Hoistway riser elevators	620.11(A) p.534	Ignition temp. of gas or vapor	501.125(A4) p.383
Hoistways, Class 2 or 3	725.136(H) p.646	Ignition temperature dusts	500.8(D2) p.375
Hollow spaces install., transformers	450.13(B) p.352	IGS cable, ampacity	T.326.80 p.191
Hollow spaces, concealed wiring	394.10 p.246	IGS cable, gas pressure 20 pounds	326.112 p.191
Hollow spaces, spread of fire	300.21 p.144	Illumination for working spaces	110.26(D) p.39
Home economics, demand	T.220.55 Note 5 p.66	Illumination, egress lighting	700.16 p.626
Hook stick, bus bar disconnect	368.17(C) p.225	Image intensifiers, X-ray	517.77 p.456
Hoops, metal, pool bonding	680.42(B) p.586	IMC conduit uses permitted	342.10 p.202
Horizontal separation	300.21 *I.N.* p.144	IMC, bends	342.26 p.202
Horsepower, controller rating	430.83 p.328	IMC, Class I, Div. I	501.10(A1a) p.376
Horsepower, disconnect rated in	430.109(A1) p.331	IMC, marking	342.120 p.203
Horsepower, plug as controller	430.81(A) p.327	IMC, standard lengths 10'	342.130 p.203
Horsepower, switch rated in	404.15(A) p.270	IMC, supports	342.30 p.203
Hosedown, motor enclosures	T.110.28 p.41	Immersion heaters	422.44 p.294
Hospital critical care, GFCI prot.	517.20(A) p.445	Immersion heaters	427.2 *I.N.* p.307
Hospital grade receptacles	517.18(B) p.444	Impedance heating	426.30 p.306
Hospital lighting demand factor	T.220.42 p.64	Impedance protected, marking	430.7 (14) p.312
Hospital, definition	517.2 p.441	Impedance requirements	517.160a *I.N. #1* p.457
Hot tubs & spas	680.40 p.586	Impedance, circuit	110.10 p.35
Hot tubs, GFCI	680.43(A2) p.587	Impedance, motor windings	430.32(B4) p.320
Hotels & motels receptacles	210.60 p.58	Impedance, transformers	T.450.3(A) p.349
House load	Example D4a p.807	Impeding heat dissipation	310.15(A3)(4) p.150
House loads	220.84(B) p.68	Impervious metal sheath cable	300.22(B) p.144
Howlers, Class III location	502.150(A1) p.390	**I.N. Informational Note**	90.5(C) p.24
Human-Caused events	708.1 *I.N. #7* p.636	In sight from,	DEF 100 p.29
Humidifer branch circuit	422.12 ex. I p.292	In sight from, A/C disconnect	440.14 p.343
Hung ceiling	300.22(C) *I.N.* p.145	In sight from, controller	430.102(A) p.330
Hybrid system,	DEF 690.2 p.594	In sight from, duct heater	424.65 p.300
Hydrochloric acids, cables	320.12(4) p.186	In sight from, motor	430.102(B1) p.330
Hydromassage bathtub, definition	680.2 p.576	In sight from, sign	600.6(A) p.520
Hydromassage bathtubs GFCI	680.71 p.590	In sight from, space heating	424.19(A1)(1) p.296
Hydromassage tub, bonding	680.74 p.590	Incandescent lamps, bases	410.103 p.285
Hydromassage units, cord	422.41 p.294	Incapacitated facilities	708.1 *I.N. #1* p.636
Hydrotherapeutic tanks	680.62 p.589	Inch-pound units	90.9(3) p.24
Hyperbaric facilities	517.34(B3) p.449	Increase heat in transformer	450.3 *I.N. #2* p.348

Entry	Reference
Increased hazards	230.95 ex.1 p.87
Indicate, its purpose identification	110.22 p.37
Individ. O.C.P. heavy-duty track	410.153 p. 289
Individual b.c. receptacles	210.21(B1) p.54
Individual branch circuit	210.3 p.48
Individual holes, boxes	314.17(C) p.180
Individual open cond., support	T.230.51(C) p.83
Individual open conductors	230.52 p.83
Individual partitions, freestanding type	605.8 p.527
Individual transformer definition	450.2 p.348
Individually or in groups, capacitor	460.25(C) p.358
Indoor antennas box barrier	810.18(C) p.683
Indoor elect. vehicle, coupling means	625.29(B) p.546
Indoor elect. vehicle, ventilation	T.625.29(D) p.546
Indoor electrical space, dedicated	110.26(E) p.39
Indoors or outdoors, arresters	280.11 p.132
Induced circulating currents	368.214 p.226
Induction coils, circulating currents	427.37 p.309
Induction coils, fixed heating	427.36 p.309
Induction generating equip.	705.40 I.N. #2 p.634
Induction heating coil over 30v	427.36 p. 309
Induction heating definition	665.2 p.567
Induction, metal raceways	300.20(A) p.144
Induction-dielectric heating	Art. 665 p.567
Inductive current, raceways	300.20(A) p.144
Inductive effect, minimized	300.20(B) p.144
Inductive lighting loads	220.18(B) p.64
Inductive reactance, differences	310.10(H1) I.N. p.149
Indust. Estab.,vertical busway riser	368.10(1)(2)p.224
Industrial control panel	409.2 p. 278
Industrial electric furnaces	Art. 665 p.567
Industrial establishments, TC cable	336.10(7) p.199
Industrial machinery clearance	110.26 p.37
Industrial machinery definition	670.2 p.572
Information Technology Equip.	Art. 645 p.559
Informational Note I.N.	90.5(C) p.24
Infrared heating lampholders	422.48(B) p.295
Infrared heating lamps	422.48 p.295
Infrared heating, overcurrent	422.11(C) p. 291
Infrastructure facilities	708.1 I.N. #1 p.636
Inherent intermittent duty	675.7 p.573
Inhibitor required, aluminum	110.14 p.36
Inner braids, cords	T.400.4 note 5 p.257
In-pound torque	110.14 I.N. p.36
Inserts, floor raceways	372.9 p.228
Inspection, heating cables	424.45 p.300
Instantaneous trip C.B., adjustable	430.52(C3) p.323
Instantaneous-trip breaker	430.52(C3) I.N. p.323
Instruction manual, untrained persons	90.1(C) p.22
Instructions for installation	110.3(B) p.35
Instrument circuit protection	727.9 p.651
Instrument transf., grd. cond.	250.178 p.129
Instrument transformers	230.82(4) p.86
Insulated busbar clearance	T.408.5 p.275
Insulated conductor, single pole	200.7(C2) p.47
Insulated fittings	300.4(G) p.137
Insulated wires marked or tagged	310.120(B) p.173
Insulating & structural appl.	110.11 I.N. #2 p.35
Insulating bushing, threaded	410.62 p.284
Insulating bushings, #4 conductor	300.4(G) p.137
Insulating joints, bonding	250.52(A1) p.111
Insulating material web, FC cable	322.2 p.188
Insulating mats motor live parts	430.233 p.335
Insulating pipe, bonding	250.52(A1) p.111
Insulating tubes	230.52 p.83
Insulation, voltage stresses	310.10(E) p.148
Insulators, clean & dry	516.10(9) p.438
Insulators, strain	225.12 p.72
Integral bonding means	314.3 ex.2 p.177
Integral component of the fixture	210.6(C2) p.50
Integral grounding shield	424.99 I.N. p. 304
Integral junction box	300.15(E) p.142
Integral parts of equipment	300.1(B) p.135
Integrated electrical systems DC	685.12 p.593
Integrated gas spacer cable	Art. 326 p.191
Integrity of electrical equipment	110.12(B) p.35
Interactive system	692.60 p.609
Interactive system, definition	690.2 p.594
Interactive systems, truck	626.27 p.551
Interbuilding cable runs	800.90 I.N. #2 p.672
Intercept lightning	800.90 I.N. #1 p.672
Interchangeable, lighting track	410.155(A) p.289
Interconnected power prod. sources	Art. 705 p.631
Interconnections, stage	520.53(J) p.465
Interior metal piping	250.68(C) p.116
Interior metal water pipe	250.68(C) p.116
Interior metal water piping	250.68(C) p.116
Interior wiring, SE cable	338.10(4) p.200
Intermediate metal conduit	342.2 p.202
Intermediate segments, rheostat	430.82(C1) p.328
Intermittent duty, motors	T.430.22(E) p.316
Internal bonding means	314.3 ex.1 p.177
Internal combustion engines	700.12(B2) p.625
Internal joiners, raceway	T.384.22 † note p.236
Internal wiring, factory installed	90.7 p.24
Interpolated, motor hp	430.6(A1) p.311
Interposed in service raceway	250.92(A2) p.117
Interrupt currents over 1200 amps	404.13(B) p.269
Interrupt of circuit, anesthetic agent	517.64 I.N. p.455
Interrupter switches, mechan. interlock	490.42 p.364
Interrupting rating	110.9 p.35
Interstices between strands	501.15 I.N. #2 p.377
Intersystem bonding dwelling	250.94 p.117
Intrinsic safety "iD"	506.2DEF p.413

Intrinsically safe circuit DEF	504.2 p.394	Junior hard service cords	T.400.4 p.254
Intrinsically safe systems	504 p.394		
Introduce noise of data errors	250.6(D) p.103		
Inverse time, circuit breaker	DEF 100 p.27	-K-	
Inverse time, circuit breaker	T.430.52 p.323		
Inverter warning label	690.5(C) p.596		
Iron, cords	422.43 p.294	Kitchen equip., feeder demand	T.220.56 p.67
Iron, flat iron	422.46 p.294	Kitchen sink, GFCI	210.8(A7) p.50
Irradiance enhancement	690.53 I.N. p.605	Kitchen waste disposers, cord	422.16(B1) p.292
Irradiated, solar	690.18 I.N. p.601	Kitchen, small appliances b.c.	210.52(B1) p.56
Irradiation, X-ray	660.23(B) p.566	Kitchen, small appliances feeder	220.52(A) p.65
Irreversible compression con.	250.64(C1) p.114	Kitchen, two 20 amp circuits	210.11(C1) p.52
Irrigation cable	675.4 p.573	Knife switches	404.6(A) p.267
Irrigation machines, B.C. rating	675.22(A) p.575	Knife switches 600 volt	404.16 p.270
Irrigation machines, ground.	675.13 p.575	Knife switches double throw	404.6(B) p.267
Irrigation machines, taps	675.10(A3) p.574	Knife switches height 6' 7"	404.8(A) p.268
Irrigation, lightning protection	675.15 p.575	Knife switches over 1200 amp	404.13(A) p.269
Island counter top receptacles	210.52(C2) p.56	Knife switches renewable contacts	404.16 p.270
Isolated by elevation 8'	430.232(3) p.335	Knob & tube wiring, extensions	394.10 p.246
Isolated conductors, color	517.160(A5) p.457	Knob and tube wiring	394.1 p.246
Isolated foreign equipment	110.26(E1b) ex. p.39	Knob and tube wiring, splices	394.56 p.247
Isolated ground receptacles	406.3(D) p.270	Knobs, glass or porcelain	225.12 p.72
Isolated grounding	250.146(D) p.127	Knobs, open wiring support	398.30 p.249
Isolated grounding circuits	250.96(B) p.118	Knockouts, close open. cabinets	312.5(A) p.174
Isolated phase installations	300.5(I) ex.2 p.139	Knockouts, closed openings boxes	314.17(A) p.179
Isolated power system, definition	517.2 p.441	Knotting the cord	400.10 I.N. p.260
Isolating switches over 600v	230.204 p.87	KVA, capacitor marking	460.12 p.358
Isolating switches, knife	404.13a p.269	KVA, vault 112 1/2	450.26 ex.1 p.353
Isolation transf., health care fac.	517.160(A4) p.457		
Isolation transformer	517.160 I.N. #1 p.457	-L-	
Isolating transformer, electric deicing	426.2 I.N. p. 304		
Isolation transformer, definition	517.2 p.441		
Isolation transformer, heating	427.26 p.309	Labeled equipment	110.3(B) p.35
ITC cable instrumentation	727.1 p.650	Ladder cable tray	392.10(B1a) p.240
ITC cable	727.10 p.651	Ladders, clearance	230.9(A) p.79
		Ladders, facilitate the raising	225.19(E) p.73
		Ladders, permanent	110.33(B) p.42
-J-		Laid on the floor, conductors	590.4(C) p.517
		Lamp bases, mogul	410.103 p.285
Jars, battery cells	480.6(B) p.360	Lamp cord	T.400.4 p.251
Joined, mechanically/electrically	110.14(B) p.36	Lamp replacement fixtures	410.142 p.288
Joints, cord tension	400.10 p.260	Lamp tie wires, fixtures	410.42 p.283
Joints, expansion	300.7(B) p.140	Lamp type "O"	410.130(F5) p.287
Joints, festoon wiring staggered	520.65 p.467	Lamp wattage marking	410.120 p.286
Joints, ground without splice	250.64(C) p.114	Lamp, electric-discharge	410.104(A) p.286
Joints, PVC conduit	352.48 p.210	Lampholder, screw shell ground	410.50 p.283
Joists, bored holes for cable	300.4(A1) p.136	Lampholder, switching device	410.93 p.285
Jumpers, bonding	250.28 p.106	Lampholders	Art. 410 p.280
Junction box from motor	430.245(A) p.336	Lampholders, admedium type	210.21(A) p.54
Junction boxes	314.28 p.183	Lampholders, candelabra-base	410.54(B) p.283
Junction boxes, accessible	314.29 p.184	Lampholders, cleat-type	410.5 ex. p.280

Term	Reference	Page
Lampholders, double-pole switched	410.93	p.285
Lampholders, dressing rooms	520.71	p.468
Lampholders, heavy-duty	210.21(A)	p.54
Lampholders, infrared	422.48(B)	p.295
Lampholders, less than 50v	720.5	p.640
Lampholders, metal to cord/bush.	410.62(A)	p.284
Lampholders, outdoor	225.24	p.73
Lampholders, over combustible area	410.12	p.281
Lampholders, pendant	410.54(A)	p.283
Lampholders, porcelain const.	410.122	p.286
Lampholders, screw-shell type	410.90	p.285
Lampholders, unswitched type	410.12	p.281
Lampholders, unswitched type	503.130(D)	p.393
Lampholders, viewing tables	530.41	p.475
Lamps, film storage vaults	530.51	p.475
Lamps, outdoor lighting	225.25	p.73
Landing stages	555.2(3)	p.513
Lanterns, stage	520.65	p.467
Lateral displacement, fixtures	501.130(B3)	p.384
Lateral, service definition	Art. 100	p.32
Laundries, wet location	300.6(D)	p.140
Laundry area, receptacle	210.52(F)	p.57
Laundry branch circuit 20 amp	210.11(C2)	p.52
Laundry facilities	Example D4a	p.807
Laundry on premises	Example D4a	p.807
Laundry outlet 6' from appliance	210.50(C)	p.55
Laundry, feeder load 1500va	220.52(B)	p.65
Laundry, no other outlets	210.11(C2)	p.52
LED drivers	220.18(B)	p.64
Lead cable, bends	300.34	p.145
Lead wire, heating cable	424.35	p.298
Lead-ins, antennas	810.18(B)	p.683
Legally req. standby systems, power	701.10	p.628
Legally required standby systems	Art. 701	p.627
Length of cord, compactors	422.16(B2)(2)	p.292
Length of cord, dishwasher	422.16(B2)(2)	p.292
Length of cord, disposers	422.16(B2)	p.292
Length of free conductor 6"	300.14	p.142
Less than 1000v grounded	250.24(C)	p.105
Letter suffixes conductors	310.120(C)	p.173
LFMC outside fittings	350.22(B)	p.207
LFNC number of conductors	356.22	p.217
Lieu of box	300.15(E)	p.142
Life safety branch, definition	517.2	p.441
Lifting handles, over 600 volts	490.38	p.363
Light aggregate	314.29 ex.	p.184
Light fixture lens, pool	680.23(5)	p.580
Light fixture, damp or wet location	410.10(A)	p.281
Light fixtures, over pool	680.22(B)	p.579
Lighting assembly, through-wall of pool	680.2	p.576
Lighting fixture, storable pool	680.33	p.586
Lighting fixtures	Art. 410	p.280
Lighting fixtures, over tub	410.10(D)	p.281
Lighting fixtures, stage	520.42	p.462
Lighting outlet, attic	210.70(A3)	p.58
Lighting outlet, attic for storage	210.70(3)	p.58
Lighting outlet, auto control	210.70(A) ex.2	p.58
Lighting outlet, basement	210.70(A3)	p.58
Lighting outlet, guest rooms	210.70(B)	p.59
Lighting outlet, heat-AC	210.70(C)	p.59
Lighting outlet, stairway	210.70(A2A)	p.58
Lighting outlet, underfloor space	210.70(A3)	p.58
Lighting outlet, utility room	210.70(A3)	p.58
Lighting outlet, vehicle door	210.70(A2B)	p.58
Lighting outlets	210.70	p.58
Lighting systems, 30v or less B.C. rating	411.6	p.290
Lighting track	410.151	p.289
Lighting track conductors	410.151(A)	p.289
Lighting track heavy-duty	410.153	p.289
Lighting track height	410.151(C8)	p.289
Lighting track interchangeable	410.151(C8)	p.289
Lighting track RMS voltage	410.151(C8)	p.289
Lighting track, 30v+ 8' from floor	410.151(C8)	p.289
Lighting, border lights	520.44	p.462
Lighting, Christmas tree	410.54(B)	p.283
Lighting, clothes closets	410.16	p.281
Lighting, cove	410.18	p.281
Lighting, egress	700.16	p.626
Lighting, emergency	700.12(A)	p.624
Lighting, exit	700.16	p.626
Lighting, festoon	225.6(B)	p.71
Lighting, means of egress	517.32(A)	p.447
Lighting, proscenium	520.44(A)	p.462
Lighting, railway conductors	110.19	p.37
Lighting, show window 200va	220.14(G)	p.62
Lighting, simulating	520.66	p.467
Lighting, track construction	410.155	p.289
Lighting, trees	410.36(G)	p.283
Lighting, vehicle lanes 12'	511.7(B1B)	p.421
Lightning arrester conductor #6	280.23	p.132
Lightning conductors, CATV	820.44(E3)	p.688
Lightning prot., irrigation mach.	675.15	p.575
Lightning rods, bonding	250.106	p.120
Lightning rods, spacing 6'	250.53(B)	p.112
Lights, dressing rooms	520.73	p.468
Limit controls, duct heater	424.64	p.300
Limit switch for hoist	610.55	p.532
Limitation, lighting voltage	210.6(A)	p.49
Limitation, voltage	300.2(A)	p.135
Limited care facility	517.2	p.441
Limited flexibilty motor connect.	501.10(A2)	p.376
Limited smoke	T.400.4 note 11	p.257
Limited-smoke characteristics	362.120	p.222
Limited-smoke LS marking	310.120(D)	p.173

Limited-smoke marking	400.6(B) p.260
Limited-smoke marking	402.9(B) p.266
Limited-smoke markings	352.120 *I.N.* p.211
Limiter, fusible connector	450.6(A3) p.351
Limiting the number of circuits	90.8(B) p.24
Line isolation monitor	517.160(B1) p.457
Line isolation monitor	517.19(E) ex. p.445
Line isolation monitor	DEF 517.2 p.441
Line monitor alarm	517.160(B) p.457
Line to neutral voltage	240.60(A2) p.97
Linear feet, show window recpt.	210.62 p.58
Linear foot, heating cable 16 1/2w	424.44(A) p.299
Linoleum, underfloor raceway	390.3(A) p.238
Liquid spillage FCC cable	324.40(A) p.189
Liquid that will burn, Class I	501.100(A1) p.381
Liquids, exposed to	110.11 p.35
Liquidtight conduit, bends	350.24 p.207
Liquidtight conduit, uses	350.10 p.207
Liquidtight flex. metal grd.	250.118(7B) p.123
Liquidtight flex. NMC, motor leads	430.245(B) p.336
Liquidtight flexible conduit	Art. 350 p.207
Liquidtight flexible conduit	553.7(B) p.512
Liquidtight, nonmetallic flex	Art. 356 p.216
Liquidtight, service	230.43(16) p.82
Listed baseboard heaters	210.52 *I.N.* p.56
Listed bushings or grommets	300.4(B1) p.136
Listed Christmas tree lighting	410.54(B) p.283
Listed equip. double insulated	250.114 ex. p.121
Listed equipment	110.3(B) p.35
Listed incandescent fixtures	210.6(C2) p.50
Listed potting compound	680.23(B2b) p.581
Listed, signs	600.3 p.519
Live parts, air space cabinet	312.11(A3) p.177
Live parts, appliances	422.4 p.290
Live parts, exposed	T.110.26(A1) p.38
Live parts, fixtures	410.5 p.280
Live parts, guarding	110.27(A) p.39
Live parts, motors	430.232 p.335
Live parts, switchboards	110.26(A1) p.38
Live parts, unguarded over 1000v	T.110.34(E) p.43
Live vegetation	225.26 p.73
Livestock facility, potential	547.10(B) *I.N. #2* p.481
Livestock is housed	547.9(C Note) p.480
Load additions existing dwellings	220.16(A1) p.63
Load balancing of circuits	210.11(B) p.51
Load diversity	310.15(B3) *I.N.* p.150
Load diversity	Table B.310.15(B)(2)(11) p.743
Load, dump	694.2 DEF p.610
Load end of service drop	250.24(A1) p.104
Load interrupters over 600v	490.21(E) p.362
Load management, services	230.94 ex.3 p.86
Load pickup, emergency systems	700.4(B) p.622
Load shedding	708.22(B) p.639
Load shedding, emergency systems	700.4(B) p.622
Loads on emergency branch cir.	700.15 p.626
Loads, dissimilar	220.60 p.65
Loads, existing dwelling	220.16(A1) p.63
Localizing a fault condition	240.12 *I.N.* p.92
Location boards, motion pictures	530.18(D) p.474
Location of lamps, outdoor lts.	225.25 p.73
Location overload units	T.430.37 p.321
Location, wet	DEF 100 p.30
Locked in open position	430.102 ex.1 p.330
Locked-rotor curr. small motor	430.110(C3) p.332
Locked-rotor current rating	440.41(A) p.344
Locked-rotor, code letter	T.430.7(B) p.313
Locknuts, double bonding	501.30(A) p.381
Longer motor acceleration	430.32(C) *I.N.* p.320
Loop wiring, cellular raceways	374.6 p.229
Loop wiring, underfloor raceways	390.7 p.239
Loop, switch white conductor	200.7(C2) p.47
Loose, rolled, or foamed insulation	394.12(5) p.247
Loudspeakers, protection	640.4 p.556
Louvers, vault door transformer	450.45(C) p.355
Low ambient condition	500.8 *I.N. #3* p.373
Low impedance grounding	250.4(B4) p.103
Low impedance path	250.4(A5) p.101
Low leakage insulation	517.160 *I.N. #1* p.457
Low-density cellulose fiberboard	410.136(B) p.288
Lower threshold value	517.160(B1) ex. p.458
Lowest temperature rating	110.14(C) p.36
Low-smoke prod. characteristics	300.22(C3) p.145
Low-smoke producing cable	725.179(A) *I.N.* p.649
Low-voltage equipment 10 volts	517.64(A1) p.455
Low-voltage systems	Art. 720 p.640
LP-gas, disconnect ground	514.11(A) p.428
Lubrication and service rooms	511.3(D3) p.421
Lugs, electrode connections	250.70 p.116
Lugs, grounding	250.70 p.116
Lugs, service conductors	230.81 p.85
Lugs, terminal connections	110.14(A) p.36
Luminaire, hanging, equipment grd.	410.42 p.283
Luminaire, lightweight to a box	314.27(A1) ex. p.182
Luminaires shower spray	410.10(D) p.281

-M-

Machine tool nameplate	670.3(A) p.572
Machine tool wire	T.310.13(A) p.168
Machine tools	Art. 670 p.572
Machines, curtain	520.48 p.463
Main bonding jumper	250.28 p.106

Main, service taps	230.46 p.82	MC cable, unsupported cables	330.30(D) p.194
Maintain concentricity note 7	T.400.4 p.257	Means of egress illumination	517.42(A) p.451
Maintenance, proper	90.1(B) p.22	Means of egress, lighting	517.32(A) p.447
Major diam. of the ellipse	Table 1 note 9 p.711	Mechanical continuity raceways	300.12 p.141
Make-or-break contacts, windings	501.105(B3) p.382	Mechanical execution of work	110.12 p.35
Malfunctioning receptacle	555.19(3) *I.N.* p.515	Mechanical execution of work	800.24 p.670
Malleable iron box	314.40(B) p.184	Mechanical protect., buried cables	300.5(D) p.139
Malleable iron, fixture studs	410.36(C) p.283	Mechanical protection, conductors	300.4 p.136
Mandatory rules shall	90.5 p.23	Mechanical protection, romex	334.15(B) p.197
Manhole, conductors	110.74 p.45	Mechanical protection, service	230.50 p. 82
Manhole control circuits	522.24 p.469	Mechanical strength for parts	110.3(A2) p. 34
Manhole covers	110.75(D) p. 45	Medium base incandescent lamps	410.103 p.285
Manhole covers, marking	110.75(E) p.45	Medium density polyethylene	326.116 p.192
Manhole covers, use of tools	110.75(D) p.45	Medium voltage cable definition	328.2 p.192
Manhole openings, ready egress	110.75(B) p.45	Medium-base HID, 277v circuit	210.6(C1) p.50
Manhole, access cover weight	110.75(D) p.45	Medium-drawn copper span 35'	810.11 ex. p.682
Manhole, round access opening	110.75 p. 45	Melting point or trip setting	230.208 p.88
Manholes, communications openings	110.75(A) p.45	Melting point or trip setting	240.100(B) p.100
Manholes, sufficient size	110.70 p.44	Mercury vapor, emergency lights	700.16 p.626
Manholes, vault, engineer. supervision	110.70 ex p.44	MESG, max. experm. safe gap	500.6(A2) p.371
Manually operable switch, feeder	225.38(A) p.75	Messenger cable, physical damage	396.12 p.248
Manually override	210.70(A1) ex.2 p.58	Messenger cable, spans over 40'	225.6(B) p.71
Manufactured build., service	545.7 p.477	Messenger supported wiring	396.2 p.247
Manufactured buildings	Art. 545 p.477	Messenger wire, festoon supports	225.6(B) p.71
Manufactured home svc. equipment	550.32(B) p.489	Metal air ducts, bonding	250.104(B) *I.N.* p.119
Manufactured wiring systems	Art. 604 p.525	Metal bands, pool bonding	680.42(B) p.586
Manufacturer's name on product	110.21 p.37	Metal box no grounding means	406.4(D2) p.271
Manufacturer's name on product	310.120(B3) p.173	Metal car frames, grounded	250.136(B) p.126
Manufacturers overload relay table	430.52(C2) p.323	Metal clad cable definition	330.2 p.193
Marinas & boatyards	Art. 555 p.512	Metal clad cable, conductor size	330.104 p.194
Marking appliances	422.60(A) p.295	Metal elbow	250.80 ex. p.116
Marking of heating cables	424.35 p.298	Metal elbow	250.86 ex.3 p.117
Marking of heating elements	422.61 p.295	Metal elbow, rigid NMC	250.80 ex. p.116
Marking tubing over 1000v	410.146 p.289	Metal embedded in floor	424.44(D) p.300
Marking, black	322.120(C) p.188	Metal enclosed busways temp. rise	368.214 p.226
Marking, motor control centers	430.98 p.329	Metal faceplates, grounded	406.6(B) p.272
Marking, phase converter	455.4 p.355	Metal faceplates, thickness	404.9(C) p.268
Marking, service equipment	230.66 p.84	Metal faceplates, thickness	406.6(A) p.272
Marquees, fixture location	410.10(A) p.281	Metal frame bldg. ground	250.136(A) p.126
Marquees, receptacles	406.8 p.272	Metal halide lamp	410.130(F5) p.287
Mast weatherhead, mobile homes	550.10(I) p.483	Metal halide, emergency lights	700.16 p.626
Mast, service	230.28 p.80	Metal hood, switchboard	520.24 p.461
Master handle, breaker	230.71(B) p.84	Metal lampholder, insulating bush.	410.62(A) p.284
Masts, stepping and unstepping	555.13(B1) p.514	Metal oxide arrester	280.4 *I.N. #2* p.132
Material handling magnet cir.	240.4(A) p.89	Metal plugs or plates, boxes	110.12(A) p.35
Material that envelops the cond.	394.12 p.247	Metal poles handhole	410.30(B) p.282
Mats or platforms for motors	430.233 p.335	Metal poles support fixtures	410.30(B) p.282
Mats, rubber for switchboards	250.174(C) p.129	Metal sheath members, CATV	800.93 p.673
MC cable definition	330.2 p.193	Metal sheaves, grounding	250.136(B) p.126
MC cable, as aerial cable	330.10(8) p.193	Metal shield connections definition	324.2 p. 189
MC cable, bending radius	330.24 p.193	Metal studs, bushing for cable	300.4(B1) p.136
MC cable, horizontal runs	330.30(C) p.194	Metal surface raceways	Art. 384 p.235

Metal underground water pipe	250.52(A1) p.111	Mobile homes, disconnect	550.11 p.483
Metal water piping bonding	250.104(A) p.119	Mobile homes, disconnect height	550.32(F) p.490
Metal well casing, grounding	250.112(M) p.121	Mobile homes, distribution system	550.30 p.489
Metal well casings	250.112(M) p.121	Mobile homes, feeder	550.33 p.490
Metal, molten arcing parts	110.18 p.37	Mobile homes, GFCI	550.13(B) p.484
Metallic interconnections	280.24(A) p.132	Mobile homes, heat tape outlet	550.13(E) p.485
Metallically isolated water pipes	250.104(A2) p.119	Mobile homes, insul. neutral	550.16(A1) p.486
Metallically joined	300.10 p.141	Mobile homes, lighting circuits	550.12(A) p.484
Metallized foil shield, signal	725.179(E) p.649	Mobile homes, portable appl.	550.2 I.N. p.481
Metal-to-metal bearing surfaces	610.61 p.532	Mobile homes, power supply	550.10 p.482
Meter loops, cabinets	312.11(C) p.177	Mobile homes, receptacles	550.13 p.484
Meter socket enclosures	230.66 p.84	Mobile homes, service	550.30 p.489
Metering equip. connections	230.46 p.82	Mobile homes, service rating	550.32 p.489
Meters, ahead of main	230.82 (2) p.85	Mobile homes, supply cord length	550.10(D) p.482
Metric units of measurement	90.9(A) p.24	Mobile homes, testing insulation	550.17 p.487
Mezzanine, access	110.33(B) p.42	Mobile homes, weatherhead	550.10(I) p.483
MG set	Example D9 p.811	Mobile homes, wiring methods	550.15 p.485
MI cable nonmagnetic sheath	300.3(B3) p.135	Mobile shovels over 600v	490.51(A) p.365
MI cable, bends	332.24 p.195	Mobile x-ray definition	517.2 p.442
MI cable, definition	332.2 p.195	Module, solar definition	690.2 p.595
MI cable, end seal	332.80 p.195	Modules, buildings	545.13 p.478
MI cable, fittings	332.40(A) p.195	Mogul base, incandescent	410.103 p.285
MI cable, ground marking	200.6(A5) p.46	Moisture-impervious metal sheath	300.50(A1) p.147
MI cable, outer sheath	332.116 p.196	Moisture-resistant NMC cable	334.116(B) p.198
MI cable, sealing	501.15 p.377	Moisture-resistant, UF cable	340.116 p.202
MI cable, solid copper	332.104 p.196	Molded case switch, motor control.	430.83(A3) p.328
MI cable, temperature limitations	332.80 p.195	Monitor hazard current	517.160(B2) I.N. p.458
MI cable, terminal seals	332.40(B) p.195	Monitor hazard current, definition	517.2 p.441
MI cable, uses permitted	332.10 p.195	Monitoring	240.12 I.N. p.92
Min. disconnecting means, feeder	225.39(D) p.76	Monorail hoists	610.21(C) p.530
Min. number branch circuits	Example D1(A) p.804	Monorail track	610.21(F) p.530
Mineral insulated cable definition	332.2 p.195	Moorage of floating buildings	555.1 p.513
Mineral insulated cable, ground	200.6(A5) p.46	Mooring lines	555.10(B) p.513
Mines, underground	90.2(B2) p.22	Motel conference room 100 persons	518.2 p.458
Minimize the effects from a short	90.8(B) p.24	Motion pict. proj., work space	540.12 p.476
Minimum cover	T.300.5 p.138	Motion picture projectors	540 p.476
Minimum radius conduit bend	Table 2 p.711	Motion picture studios feeders	530.18(B) p.474
Minor relative motions	545.13 p.478	Motor control center grounding	430.96 p.329
Minus 10° C (plus 14° F)	310.10 I.N. p.147	Motor control center, barriers	430.97(E) p.329
Minus 10° C (plus 14° F)	402.3 I.N. p.262	Motor control centers	430.92 p.329
Mirror frames	680.43(D4) ex. p.587	Motor control circuit, Definition	430.2 p.311
Mobile equip., grd. electrode	250.188(E) p.131	Motor control units	430.98(B) p.329
Mobile equipment, DEF	513.2 p.422	Motor controller, molded case switch	430.83(A3) p.32
Mobile high volt. equip., ground cond.	250.190 p.131	Motor controller, outdoor submerged	T.110.28 p.41
Mobile home, definition	550.2 p.481	Motor disconnect, attachment plug	430.109(F) p.331
Mobile home, primary protector	800.106 p.675	Motor disconnect, higher than 6' 7"	404.8 ex.#2 p.268
Mobile homes & parks	Art. 550 p.481	Motor driven appliance, disconnect	422.35 p.294
Mobile homes, appliances	550.12(D) p.484	Motor installation, capacitor	460.9 & 10 p.357
Mobile homes, bonding	550.16(C) p.487	Motor protection, over 600v	430.225 ex. p.334
Mobile homes, branch circuit	550.12 p.484	Motor starting current	430.52(B) p.322
Mobile homes, calculations	550.18 p.487	Motor-comp. controller	440.41(B) p.345
Mobile homes, demand factors	550.31 p.489	Motor-comp. plug rating	440.55(B) p.346

Motor-compressor time delay	440.54(B) p.346	Motors, feeder taps	430.28 p.318
Motor-generator equipment	665.10(B) p.567	Motors, future additions	430.62(B) p.325
Motors	Art. 430 p.310	Motors, general use snap switch	430.109(C2) p.331
Motors, accidental ground	430.74 p.326	Motors, grounding	430.241 p.335
Motors, accidental starting	430.74 p.326	Motors, guards for attendants	430.233 p.335
Motors, adjustable speed drive	430.2 p.310	Motors, hazard to persons	430.225(A) ex. p.334
Motors, armature shunt resistors	430.29 p.319	Motors, heater sizing maximum	430.32(C) p.320
Motors, attachment plug rating	430.42(C) p.322	Motors, heater sizing minimum	430.32(A) p.319
Motors, automatic restarting	430.43 p.322	Motors, heavy-capacity feeders	430.62(B) p.325
Motors, automatic starting	430.35(B) p.321	Motors, highest locked-rotor	430.7(B3) p. 312
Motors, autotransformer	430.82(B) p.328	Motors, highest rated	430.17 p.316
Motors, auxiliary leads	T.430.12(B) notes p.315	Motors, hi-voltage O.C.P.	430.225(C1a) p.334
Motors, branch circuit	430.22 p.316	Motors, large-capacity inst.	430.62(B) p.325
Motors, branch circuit O.C.P.	T.430.52 p.323	Motors, letter code table	T.430.7(B) p.313
Motors, brush rigging	430.232 ex. p.335	Motors, limited flexibility	501.10(B2) p.377
Motors, bushing	430.13 p.315	Motors, live parts	430.232 p.335
Motors, can be started kva	430.7(B1) p. 313	Motors, locked in open	430.102(B) ex. p.330
Motors, capacitors	430.27 p.318	Motors, locked-rotor	430.7(B) p.312
Motors, clock	430.32(B4) *I.N.* p.320	Motors, locked-rotor current	430.110(C3) p.332
Motors, code letter	T. 430.7(B) p.313	Motors, marked diameter	430.7(A12) p.312
Motors, collector rings	430.14(B) p.316	Motors, mats or platforms	430.233 p.335
Motors, combination load	430.25 p.318	Motors, molded case switch	430.109(A3) p.331
Motors, combined protection	430.55 p.325	Motors, multispeed	430.7(B1) p.313
Motors, commutators	430.14(B) p.316	Motors, nameplate	430.7(A) p.312
Motors, conductor fuses	430.36 p.321	Motors, next higher size	430.52(C1)ex 1 p.322
Motors, contact arm	430.82(C1) p.328	Motors, nonautomatically	430.35(A) p.320
Motors, continuous duty	T.430.22(E) note p.317	Motors, noncombustible housings	430.12(A) ex. p.314
Motors, control circuit torque	430.9(C) p.314	Motors, nonventilated enclosed	503.125 p.393
Motors, control circuits	430.71 p.326	Motors, occasional prolonged sub.	T.110.28 p.41
Motors, control transformer	430.75(B) p.327	Motors, oil switch	430.111(B3) p.332
Motors, controllers	430.81 p.327	Motors, open	430.14(B) p.316
Motors, controllers rating	T.110.28 p.41	Motors, orderly shutdown	430.44 p.322
Motors, cord & plug connected	430.42(C) p.322	Motors, over 600 volts	430.221 p.334
Motors, DC contant voltage	430.29 p.318	Motors, overload sizing	430.32 p.319
Motors, DC fractional	430.7(A12) p.312	Motors, overload units	T.430.37 p.321
Motors, disconnect	430.101 p.330	Motors, pipe-ventilated	430.16 *I.N.* p.316
Motors, disconnect 100 hp	430.109(D) p.331	Motors, pipe-ventilated	503.125 p.393
Motors, disconnect amp rating	430.110(A) p.331	Motors, portable 1/3 hp	430.81(B) p.327
Motors, disconnect rated in hp	430.109(C) p.331	Motors, power & light loads	430.63 p.325
Motors, dust accumulation	430.16 p.316	Motors, prot. live parts	430.231 p.335
Motors, duty-cycle	T.430.22(E) p.317	Motors, rating of plug	430.42(C) p.322
Motors, dynamic braking	430.29 p.318	Motors, rectifier voltage	430.18 p.316
Motors, enclosed pos. pressure vent.	501.125(A2) p.383	Motors, resistor duty	T.430.23(C) p.317
Motors, escalator	620.61(B2) p.542	Motors, rheostats	430.82(C) p.328
Motors, exciting fields	T.430.12(B) note p.315	Motors, second. cir. wound-rotor	430.32(E) p.320
Motors, exposure to dust	430.16 p.316	Motors, separation of junct. box	430.245(B) p.336
Motors, factory connections	430.12(D) p.314	Motors, service factor	430.32(A1) p.319
Motors, fan cooled	503.125 p.393	Motors, shaded-pole	440.6(B) p.341
Motors, fault-current prot.	430.225(C) p.334	Motors, shunting	430.35 p.320
Motors, feeder conductors sizing	430.24 p.318	Motors, simultaneously disc.	430.225(C1a) p.334
Motors, feeder demand	430.26 p.318	Motors, single-phase F.L.C.	T.430.248 p.337
Motors, feeder protection sizing	430.62 p.325	Motors, sparks	430.14(B) p.316

Motors, split-capacitor	440.6(B) p.341
Motors, split-phase	430.32(B4) *I.N.* p.320
Motors, stage curtains	520.48 p.463
Motors, stationary 2 hp	430.109(C) p.331
Motors, stationary frame grd.	430.242 p.335
Motors, temperature rise	430.32(A1) p.319
Motors, terminal housings	430.12(A) p.314
Motors, terminal spacing	T.430.12(C1) p.315
Motors, three-phase F.L.C.	T.430.250 p.338
Motors, torque	430.7(C) p.313
Motors, torque requirements	430.9(C) p. 314
Motors, totally enclosed	501.125(A2) p.383
Motors, usable volumes	T.430.12(C2) p.315
Motors, ventilation	430.14(A) p.315
Motors, voltage rating	430.83(E) p.328
Motors, winding impedance	430.32(B4) p.320
Motors, wire bending space	T.430.10(B) p.314
Motors, wire-to-wire connect.	T.430.12(B) p.315
Motors, wooden floors	430.14(B) ex. p.316
Motors, wound-rotor	430.23(A) p.317
Motors, wound-rotor secondaries	430.32(E) p.320
Motors. D.C. F.L.C.	T.430.247 p.336
Mounting of boxes	314.23(A) p.180
Mounting of equipment	110.13(A) p.35
Mounting of fixtures	410.30 p.282
Mounting of switches	404.10 p.268
Mounting yoke	404.10(B) p.268
Moving walks	Art. 620 p.532
Multi-car installations, elevators	620.52(A) p.541
Multicircuit track fixtures	410.151 p.289
Multiconductor cable, tunnel	110.53 p.44
Multiconductor portable cables	400.30 p.261
Multifamily dwelling, optional	T.220.84 p.69
Multioutlet assemblies	220.14(H) p.63
Multioutlet assembly, thru dry partition	380.76 p.233
Multi-outlet BC, plug connect. loads	210.19(A2) p.53
Multiple branch circuits same yoke	210.7 p.50
Multiple DC voltages	690.8(C) p.598
Multiple electrodes spacing	250.53(B) p.112
Multiple raceways grounding	250.122(C) p.124
Multisection enclosures	501.125(B) *I.N. #2* p.384
Multiwire branch circuits	210.4 p.48
Multiwire branch circuits	501.40 p.381
Multiwire branch circt. PV 120v warn.	690.10(C) p.599
MV cable 35kv, uses permitted	328.10 p.192
MV cable definition	328.2 p.192

-N-

Nacelle, Definition	694.2 p.610
Nails to mount knobs 10 penny	398.30(D) p.250
National security disrupt	708.1 *I.N. #1* p.636
Natural draft ventilation system	668.40 p.571
Natural gas rated pipe	326.116 p.192
Navigable water, wiring	555.9 p.513
Neat and workmanlike manner	110.12 p. 35
Neon conductor length	600.32(J1) p.524
Neon tubing	600.41 p.524
Network powered broadband DEF	830.2 p.695
Network powered broadband comm. syst.	Art. 830 p.695
Network-power. broadband pool clear.	680.8(C) p.577
Neutral can be reduced	551.72 p.501
Neutral conductor	310.15(B5a) p.152
Neutral conductor routing	250.36(D) p.111
Neutral conductor, branch circuit	200.4 p.46
Neutral conductor, cords	400.5 p.258
Neutral fully insulated	250.36(B) p.111
Neutral grounding impedance	250.36(C) p. 111
Neutral, ampacity solar	705.95 p.635
Neutral, autotrn. phase current	450.5 *I.N.* p.350
Neutral, bare service	230.22 ex. p.79
Neutral, boiler over 600v	490.72(E) p.366
Neutral, bonding to service	250.92(B) p.117
Neutral, busway	368.258 p.226
Neutral, carry the unbalance	310.15(5)a p.152
Neutral, clothes dryer feeder 70%	220.61 p.67
Neutral, cook. equip. B.C.	210.19(A3) ex 2 p.53
Neutral, cook. equip. feeder 70%	220.61 p.67
Neutral, feeder load	220.61 p.67
Neutral, feeders	215.4 p.60
Neutral, insul., mobile homes	550.11(A) p.483
Neutral, min. insulation level	250.184(A) p.129
Neutral, minimum service size	250.24(BC1) p.105
Neutral, outside wiring	225.7(B) p.71
Neutral, portable switchboards	520.51 p.464
Neutral, reduction feeder	220.61(B) p.67
Neutral, solidly grounded	250.184 p.129
Neutral, solid-state dimmers	520.25(D) p.461
Next higher O.C.P. device	240.4(B) p.90
NFPA Regulations Gov. Committe	90.6 p.24
Night club lighting dimmer	520.25(A) p.461
Nipple, 24" & 60% fill	Chapter 9 note 4 p.711
Nipple, derating factor	T.310.15(B3A)(2) p.152
NM cable unsupported	334.30(B) p.197
NM Cable, in dropped or suspend. ceil.	334.12(A2) p.196
NM cable, protection	334.15(B) p.197
NM cable, supports	334.30 p.197
NM Cable, temporary wiring	590.4(B & C) p.517
NM cable, uses	334.10 p.196
NMC cable, construction	334.100 p.198
NMC cable, definition	334.116(B) p.198
NMS cable, power conductors	334.116(C) p.198

Entry	Reference
No appliances and no lamps	700.15 p.626
No equipment ground	406.4(D2B) p.271
No heating due to hysteresis	300.20(B) *I.N.* p.144
No point along the floor line 6'	210.52(A1) p.56
Nominal battery voltage definition	480.2 p.359
Nonautomatically started motor	430.35(A) p.320
Nonbridge structures, clearance	225.19(B) p.73
Nonbuilding	225.19(B) p.73
Noncapacitive load, signal	725.41(A2) p.642
Noncarbon arc discharge lamp	530.17(B) p.473
Noncinder concrete	342.10(C) p.202
Noncohesive granulated soil	314.29 ex. p.184
Noncoincident loads, omit smaller	220.60 p. 65
Noncombustible cases, lamps	410.104(A) p.286
Nonconductive coatings, removed	250.12 p.103
Nonconductive paint, bonding	250.96(A) p.118
Nonconductive rope operator	668.32(B2) p.571
Nonconductive, optical fiber	770.2 p.660
Noncontinuous load, plus cont.	230.42(A1) p.82
Nonferrous metal, electrodes	250.52(A6) p.112
Nonfire-rated floor/ceiling	300.11(A2) p.141
Nonflammable dielectric fluid	450.24 p.353
Non-GFCI protect., dwell. garage	210.8(A3) ex. p.50
Non-grid-interactive systems	692.59 p.609
Nongrounding type receptacles	406.4(D2) p.271
Nonheating leads, cables length	424.34 p.298
Nonhygroscopic, irrigation cable	675.4(A) p.573
No-niche fixture	680.23(D) p.581
Nonincendive circuit	500.2 p.368
Nonincendive circuits	501.10(B3) p.377
Nonincendive circuits	501.10(B3) p.377
Nonincendive circuits	502.10(B3) p.377
Nonincendive field wiring	500.2 p.367
Noninsulated busbar clearance	T.408.5 p. 275
Noninterchangeable cartridge fuse	240.60(B) p.97
Noninterchangeable S fuse	240.53(B) p.96
Nonlinear loads	400.5 p.258
Nonlinear loads	210.4(A) *I.N.* p.48
Nonlinear loads	220.61 p.67
Nonlinear loads	310.15(5)c p.152
Nonlinear loads	450.3 *I.N. #2* p.348
Nonlinear loads	DEF 100 p.30
Nonmagnetic sheath	300.3(B3) p.135
Nonmagnetic sheath MI cable	300.3(B3) p.135
Nonmedical or nondental, X-ray	660.1 p.565
Nonmetallic box, clamps	334.30 p.197
Nonmetallic boxes, supports	314.23 p.180
Nonmetallic boxes, uses	314.3 p.177
Nonmetallic extensions definition	382.2 p.233
Nonmetallic fillers, cables	T.400.4 note 7 p.257
Nonmetallic frames, space heat	424.44(C) p. 300
Nonmetallic raceways, HealthCare	517.30(C3)(2) p.447
Nonmetallic surface extensions	382.2 p. 233
Nonmetallic wireways	378.2 p.231
Nonmetallic wireways, sunlight	378.12(3) p.231
Nonmetallic wireways, supports	378.30 p.232
Nonmetallic wiring, bulk plant	515.8(C) p.433
Nonmetallic-sheathed cable	Art. 334 p.196
Nonmotor appliance overcurrent	422.11(E) p.291
Nonorderly shutdown	230.95 ex. p.87
Nonplasticized PVC	362.100 p.222
Nonpower-limited fire circuit	336.10(6) p.199
Nonpower-limited fire signaling	760.41(A) p.652
Nonremovable S fuse adapters	240.54(C) p.96
Nonshielded conductors	300.3(C1) p. 136
Nonshielded conductors	310.10(E) ex. p.148
Nonshielded high-voltage cables	300.50(A2) p.147
Nontamperable circuit breaker	240.82 p.97
Nontamperable S fuse	240.54(D) p.96
Non-type IC, minimum clearance	410.116(A1) p.286
Nonwicking filler, machines	675.4(A) p.573
Notches in wood	300.4(A2) p.136
NPLFP cable	760.53(B1) p.654
NPLFP cable, fire signal	760.176(C) p.658
NPT conduit cutting die	500.8(E) p.375
NPT threads 5	500.8(E1) p.375
NUCC trimming	354.28 p.213
Number of bends in one run	344.26 p.204
Number of circuits in enclosures	90.8(B) p.24
Number of cond. in conduit	640.23(A) p.558
Number of conductors in conduit	Annex C p.744
Number of disconnects, feeder	225.33(A) p.74
Nurses' stations, definition	517.2 p.441
Nursing home, definition	517.2 p.441

-O-

Entry	Reference
O.C.P. readily accessible location, feeder	225.40 p.76
O.C.P., continuous and non loads	210.20(A) p.53
Objectionable current, grounding	250.6(A) p.103
Oblique angle, ground rod	250.53(G) p.113
Occupancy sensors, photocell	210.70(A) ex.2 p.58
Office furnishings, recpt. outlet	605.5(C) p.526
Office, partition plug & cord	605.8 p.527
Office, unknown receptacles	220.14(K) p.63
Offset, enclosures	312.6(B) *I.N.* p.175
OFN & OFC cables	770.179(D) p.668
OFNP & OFCP cables	770.179(A) p.666
OFNR & OFCR cables	770.179(B) p.666
Oil circuit breakers	490.21(A1c) p.361
Oil switch service disconnect	230.204(A) p.87
Oil switch, motor	430.111(B3) p.332

Oil-filled cutouts	490.21(D) p.362	Optical fiber cables, nonconductive	770.2 p.660
Oil-fired central heating	550.10(A) ex.1 p.482	Optical fiber cables, point of entry	770.2 DEF p.660
One conductor diameter, spacing	370.4(D) p. 227	Optical fibers, raceways	90.2(A) p.22
One conductor per ground clamp	250.70 p.116	Optical network terminal, ONT	840.2 DEF p.707
One neutral several circuits	215.4(A) p.60	Optical power supply unit, OPSU	840.1 I.N. p.707
One outlet for sign-outline light.	600.5(A) p.519	Optional calculation, add. loads	220.87 p.69
One shot bender	Table 2 Chapt. 9 p.711	Optional calculation, dwelling unit	220.82 p.67
One wire under screw terminal	110.14(A) p.36	Optional calculation, exist. dwelling	220.83 p.68
ONT (optical network terminal)	840.2 Def. p.707	Optional calculation, multi-dwelling	220.84 p.68
Open circuit voltage dwelling	410.139(B) p.288	Optional calculation, restaurant	220.88 p.70
Open conductor	230.52 p.83	Optional calculation, school	220.86 p.69
Open motors with commutators	430.14(B) p.316	Optional markings	310.120(D) p.173
Open or partially enclosed lamps	410.16(B) p.281	Optional standby systems	700.4 (B) p.622
Open porches, canopies, marquees	406.9(A) p.272	Orange triangle, receptacles	406.3(D) p.270
Open service conductors supports	T.230.51(C) p.83	Orderly shutdown, elect. system	240.12 p.92
Open spraying classification	516.3(C1) p.435	Orderly shutdown, integrated sys.	685.1 p.592
Open wire systems on insulators	398.10 p.248	Orderly shutdown, motor	430.44 p.322
Open wire systems on insulators	404.10(A) p.268	Organ, conductor size	650.6(A) p.565
Open wiring, accessible attics	394.23 p.247	Organ, overcurrent protection	650.8 p.565
Open wiring, conductor separation	225.14(C) p.72	Organ, rectifier grounding	650.4 p.564
Open wiring, conductor support	398.30 p. 249	Organic coatings boxes raintight	300.6(A2) p. 140
Open wiring, dead end connection	398.30(A2) p.249	Organic materials	300.6(A2) p.140
Open wiring, maximum voltage 600v	225.10 p.72	Ornamental pools	680.2 p.576
Open wiring, porcelain supports	225.12 p.72	Oscillator-type units, induct. heat	665.2 p.567
Open wiring, running boards	398.23(A) p.249	Outbuildings snap sw. disconnect	225.36 ex. p.75
Open-circuit voltage 1000 or less	410.130(A) p. 286	Outdoor antenna conductor	T.810.16(A) p.683
Open-circuit voltage lighting track	410.151(C8) p.289	Outdoor installations	Art. 225 p.71
Open-circuit voltage over 1000v	410.140(A) p.288	Outdoor lampholders, puncture wire	225.24 p.73
Open-circuit voltage over 300v	410.135 p. 287	Outdoor lighting	Art. 225 p.71
Open-conductor, separation	225.14(C) p.72	Outdoor lighting trees	410.36(G) p.283
Open-conductor, spacing	225.14 p.72	Outdoor overhead cond. over 600v	Art. 399 p.250
Open-conductor, supports	225.12 p.72	Outdoor port. signs, power cord	600.10(C2) p.522
Open-conductors, clearance	225.18 p.72	Outdoor portable signs, GFCI	600.10(C2) p.522
Open-conductors, final spans	225.19(D) p.73	Outdoor receptacles	210.52(E) p.57
Open-conductors, on insulators	225.12 p.72	Outdoor swimming pool,	DEF 680.2 p.576
Open-conductors, on poles spacing	225.14(D) p.72	Outdoor trench, derating fact.	310.15(B3a)(3) p.152
Open-conductors, over 600v clear.	T.490.24 p.364	Outdoor type boxes	300.6(A) p.139
Open-conductors, porcelain-knobs	225.12 p.72	Outer screw-shell terminal	210.6(C2) p.50
Open-conductors, protection	225.20 p.73	Outer sheath properties, cords	400.9 p. 260
Open-conductors, service drops	230.22 p.79	Outlet boxes to be covered	410.22 p.282
Openings to be closed, boxes	314.17(A) p.179	Outlet boxes, listed for weight	410.30(A) p.282
Openings to be closed, cabinets	312.5(A) p.174	Outlet boxes, support 50 pounds	314.27(A2) p.183
Openings to be closed, equip.	110.12(A) p.35	Outlet cabled, communications	800.156 p.678
Operating handle switch height	404.8(A) p.268	Outlet, appliance	210.50(C) p.55
Operating handles, 50 pounds	490.41(A) ex. p.364	Outlet, heat tape	550.13(E) p.485
Operating valves, motors	T.430.22(E) p.317	Outlets, abandoned	390.8 p.239
Operation at standstill, motors	430.7(C) p.313	Outlets, discontinued	374.7 p.229
Opposite polarity spacing	T.408.56 p.277	Outlets, discontinued	390.8 p.239
OPSU (optical power supply unit)	840.1 I.N. p.707	Outlets, dwelling	210.52 p.55
Optical density, signal ciruit	725.179 I.N. p.649	Outlets, flush with finish	314.20 p.180
Optical fiber cables	Art. 770 p.660	Outlets, laundry	210.52(F) p.57
Optical fiber cables, conductive	770.2 p.660	Outlets, required	210.50 p.55

Outlets, tree lighting	410.36(G) p.283
Outline lighting, disconnect	600.6 p.520
Output circuit, induction heating	665.5 p.567
Outside branch circuits	Art. 225 p.71
Outside dimensions floor area	220.12 p.61
Outside feeders	Art. 225 p.71
Outside, common neutral	225.7(B) p.71
Outside, conductor covering	225.4 p.71
Outside, overhead spans	225.6(A) p.71
Outside, service considered, concrete	230.6(2) p.79
Outside, service disconnect	230.70(A) p.84
Outside, wiring on bldgs.	225.10 p.72
Oven receptacles	210.52(B2) ex.2 p.56
Ovens, cord connected	422.16(B3) p.292
Ovens, feeder demand	T.220.55 p.66
Over 600 v, nonshielded cables	300.50(A2) p.147
Over 600 volts	Art. 490 p.360
Over 600v, clearance live parts	T.490.24 p.364
Over 600v, electrode boilers	490.70 p.366
Over 600v, minimum cover	T.300.50 p.146
Over 600v, motor B.C. conductors	430.224 p.334
Over 600v, resistors & reactors	470.18(B) p.359
Overcurrent device phys. damage	240.24(C) p.95
Overcurrent device, vertical pos.	240.33 p.96
Overcurrent devices, clothes closet	240.24(D) p.95
Overcurrent devices, readily acc.	240.24(A) p.95
Overcurrent devices, wet location	240.32 p.95
Overcurrent prot, feeder over 600v	240.100 p.100
Overcurrent prot, location from arc	240.41(A) p.96
Overcurrent prot. fixture wire	240.5(B2) p.91
Overcurrent prot., bathrooms	240.24(E) p.95
Overcurrent prot., capacitors	460.25(C) p.358
Overcurrent prot., Class I Div. 2	501.115(B) p. 382
Overcurrent prot., electroplating	669.9 p.572
Overcurrent prot., emerg. systems	700.25 p.627
Overcurrent prot., indust. mach.	670.4(B) p.572
Overcurrent prot., motors b.c.	T.430.52 p.323
Overcurrent prot., second. ties	450.6(B) p.351
Overcurrent prot., transformer	T.450.3(A) p.349
Overcurrent protect., readily acc.	240.10 p.91
Overcurrent protection, appliances	422.11 p.291
Overcurrent protection, Class 1	725.43 p.642
Overcurrent protection, DC gen.	530.63 p.475
Overcurrent protection, dimmers	520.25(A) p.461
Overcurrent protection, fire cir.	760.43 p.652
Overcurrent protection, hazard	240.4(A) p.89
Overcurrent protection, location	240.21 p.92
Overcurrent protection, organ	650.8 p.565
Overcurrent protection, taps	240.4(E) p.90
Overcurrent protection, welders	630.12(A) p.552
Overcurrent	DEF 100 p.30
Overcurrent, infrared heating	422.11(C) p.291
Overcurrent, nonmotor appl.	422.11(E) p.291
Overcurrent, plugging boxes	530.18(D) p.474
Overcurrent, trip unit	240.15(A) p.92
Overhead feeders house to garage	225.6(A1) p.71
Overhead gantry	626.23 p.549
Overhead service conductors	230.22 p.79
Overhead service drop clear. pool	680.8 p.577
Overhead service drop, bare	230.22 ex. p.79
Overhead spans	225.6(A) p.71
Overheating receptacle	555.19(A3) I.N. p.515
Overload protection-combined, motors	430.55 p.325
Overload relay, class 20 or 30	430.32(C) I.N. p.320
Overload sizing, motors	430.32 p.319
Overload units location	T.430.37 p.321
Overloads required for 3ø	T.430.37 p.321
Over-pressure limit control	424.74 page 301
Oversized knockouts	250.97 ex. p.118
Oversized sleeve	555.13(B4)(a5) p.514
Over-temperature limit control	424.73 p.301
Ozone-resistant insulation	310.10(E) p.148

-P-

Paddle fan, box	314.27(D) p. 183
Paddle fan, height over pool	680.22(B1) p. 579
Paddle fan, height over spa	680.43(B1b) p.587
Paddle fans, box support	314.27(D) p.183
PAF & PTF wire types	760.49(C) ex. p.653
Paint	110.12(B) p.35
Paint containers, grounded	516.10(A6) p.438
Paint, gooseneck service head	230.54(B) p.83
Paint, wallpaper, finished ceilings	424.42 p.299
Paint, white wire	200.7(A) p.47
Paired fixture sections	410.137(C) p.288
Pan boxes	314.25(B) p.182
Panel sets under floor covering	424.99(B) p.304
Panelbds., mounted above or below	110.26(A3) p.38
Panelboard as service, bonding	408.3(C) p.274
Panelboard bonding, health care	517.14 p.443
Panelboard, back-fed	408.36(D) p.276
Panelboard, ceiling clearance	408.18(A) p.275
Panelboard, clearance working	110.26(A) p.38
Panelboard, conductors spliced	312.8 p.175
Panelboard, dead front	408.38 p.276
Panelboard, dedicated space	110.26(E) p.39
Panelboard, grounding	408.40 p.276
Panelboard, high-leg marking	110.15 p.36
Panelboard, illumination	110.26(D) p.39

Entry	Reference
Panelboard, individual prot.	408.36 ex.1 p.276
Panelboard, located over appliance	110.26(A3) p.38
Panelboard, min. spacing parts	T.408.56 p.277
Panelboard, multiwire branch circuit	210.4 p.48
Panelboard, not as a junction box	312.8 p.175
Panelboard, opposite polarity	T.408.56 p.277
Panelboard, overcurrent protection	408.36 p.276
Panelboard, phase arrangement	408.3(E) p. 274
Panelboard, pool	680.25 p.583
Panelboard, raceway end fitting	408.5 p.275
Panelboard, rating	408.30 p.276
Panelboard, rec. vehicle	551.45 p.495
Panelboard, splices in not allowed	312.8 p.175
Panelboard, sprinkler protect.	110.26(E1c) p.39
Panelboard, switches 30a or less	408.36(A) p.276
Panelboard, used as service	408.3(C) p.274
Panelboard, wet location 1/4" air	312.2(A) p.174
Panelboard, wet or damp location	408.16 p.275
Panelboard, working clearance	110.26(A) p.38
Panelboards	Art. 408 p.274
Panelboards, close proximity	408.56 p.277
Panelboards, column width	300.3(B4) p.135
Panic bars, open in direction of egress	110.26(C3) p.39
Panic bars, transformer doors	450.43(C) p.354
Pans, fixture	410.23 p.282
Pantry, small appliance	210.52(B1) p.56
Paper spacer thickness, gas cable	T.326.112 p.191
Paperlined lampholders	410.82(B1) p.285
Parallel power prod. systems	230.2(A5) p.78
Parallel to framing members	300.4(D) p.137
Parallel to joists, studs, rafters	330.17 p.193
Parallel, #1/0 conductors	310.10(H) p.148
Parallel, #20 or larger wire	620.12(A1) p.535
Parallel, elevator lighting	620.12(A1) p.535
Parallel, fuses or breakers	240.8 p.91
Parallel, transformers	450.7 p.351
Parallel, traveling cables	620.12(A1) p.535
Park trailer, exposed cord	552.44(B) p.506
Park trailer, lighting switches	552.52(A) p.510
Parking garages, fuel	511.1 p.419
Parts, broken; bent; cut	110.12(B) p.35
Part-winding motors	430.4 p. 311
Passenger station	110.19 ex. p.37
Patch panel, theater	520.50 p.463
Patching tables, lampholders	530.41 p.475
Patient bed receptacles	517.18(B) p.444
Patient care area, definition	517.2 p.441
Patient equip. ground. point	517.19(C) I.N. p.444
Patient vicinity, definition	517.2 p.442
Patient vicinty, exposed surfaces	517.11 p.442
Paving, earth access to box	314.29 p.184
Peak load shaving	708.22(B) p.639
Peak load shaving, emergency	700.4(B) p.622
Pediatric location receptacles	517.18(C) p.444
Pendant boxes, strain relief	314.23(H1) p.181
Pendant cond., twisted or cabled	410.54(C) p.283
Pendant conductors, size	410.54(B) p.283
Pendant fixtures, Class I location	501.130(A3) p.384
Pendant fixtures, closets	410.16(C) p.281
Pendant lampholders, support	410.54(A) p. 283
Pendant pushbutton, plating	668.32(B3) p.571
Pendants bathtub rim	410.10(D) p.281
Penetrations are made	300.21 I.N. p.144
Peninsular counter top receptacles	210.52(C3) p.56
Periodic duty, motors	T.430.22(E) p.317
Permanent amusement attraction	Art. 522 p.468
Permanent barriers, separate box	314.28(D) p.183
Permanent ladders or stairways	110.33(B) p.42
Permanent ladders, access	110.33(B) p.42
Permanent moisture level, electro.	250.53(A1) p.112
Permanent plaque	230.2(E) p.79
Permanent plaque or directory, feeder	225.37 p.75
Permanently installed feeder	550.10(A) p.482
Permissive rules	90.5(B) p.24
Personnel doors	110.26(C3) p.39
Persons who are not qualified	110.31 p.40
Persons, 100 or more assembly	518.1 p.458
Persons, untrained	90.1(C) p.22
Phase arrangement	430.97(B) p.329
Phase arrangement panelboard	408.3(E) p. 274
Phase convert. H.P. rated disconnect	455.8(C2) p.356
Phase converter marking	455.4 p.355
Phase converter O.C.P.	455.7 p.356
Phase converter O.C.P. fixed loads	455.7(B) p.356
Phase converter O.C.P. variable	455.7(A) p.356
Phase converter, ampacity	455.6(A) p.355
Phase converter, capacitors	455.23 p.357
Phase converter, motors	455.2 I.N. p.355
Phase converter, power interruption	455.22 p.357
Phase converter, start-up	455.21 p.356
Phase converters	Art. 455 p.355
Phase converters, static & rotary	455.2 p.355
Phase fault protection over 600v	490.72(C) p.366
Photo cell controlled	210.70(A) ex. 2 p.58
Photovoltaic arrays, ground fault protect	690.5 p.596
Photovoltaic bus bar rating 120%	705.12(D2) p.632
Photovoltaic DC circuits in bldg. metal race.	690.31(E) p.60
Photovoltaic disable an array	690.18 p.601
Photovoltaic disconnect shall not break ground	690.13 p.599
Photovoltaic disconnecting means marking	690.14(C2) p.600
Photovoltaic equipment grounding	690.43 p.603
Photovoltaic grounding electrode AC & DC	690.47(C) p.60
Photovoltaic latching/locking connectors, tool	690.33(C) p.60
Photovoltaic modules, solar	690.18 I.N. p.601

Photovoltaic modules volt. corr. factor	T.690.7 p.597
Photovoltaic moving parts of tracking PV	690.31(C) p.601
Photovoltaic power source, grounded	690.41 p.603
Photovoltaic source circuit, current x 125%	690.8(A1) p.597
Photovoltaic source circuits AC modules	690.6(A) p.596
Photovoltaic storage batteries dwelling	690.71(B) p.605
Photovoltaic system batt. warning label	690.5(C) p.596
Photovoltaic system currents are continuous	690.8(B) p.598
Photovoltaic system maximum voltage	690.7(A) p.597
Phychiatric hospital, definition	517.2 p.442
Physical damage, conductors	300.4 p.136
Physical environment de-icing	426.10 (1) p.305
Piercing a floor, pool cord	680.22(A5) p.579
Piers, receptacles	555.19 p.515
Pig tail required to device	300.13(B) p.141
Pilot light circuit protection	408.52 p.277
Pilot light, conductors	520.53(G) p.464
Pilot light, receptacle	520.73 p.468
Pilot light, stage	520.53(G) p.464
Pipe heating assemblies	422.50 p.295
Pipe organ, source of power	650.4 p.564
Pipe organs, wire size	650.6(A) p.564
Pipeline, definition	427.2 p.307
Piping without valves	500.5(B2) I.N. #2 p.370
Pit or depression, garages	511.3(C3)(B) p.420
Pit, aircraft hangar	513.3(A) p.422
Pit, spray application	516.3(C) p.435
Place of assembly, bowling lanes	518.2(A) p.458
Places of assembly	518.1 p.458
Places of assembly, wiring meth.	518.4 p.459
Plans, feeder diagram	215.5 p.60
Plant hardiness zone	626.11 I.N. p.548
Plaque shall be posted	230.72(A) ex. p.85
Plaque, service directory	230.2(E) p.79
Plaster	110.12(B) p.35
Plaster ears, switches	404.10(B) p.268
Plaster or plasterboard repairs	314.21 p.180
Plaster rings, box	314.16(A) p.178
Plastic materials	110.11 I.N. #2 p.35
Plate electrodes, 2 sq.ft.	250.52(A7) p.112
Platforms, access	110.33(B) p.42
Plenum cable	T.725.154(G) p.648
Plenum	DEF 100 p.31
Plenum, cables	725.154a p.647
Plenums, type BLP	T.830.154(B) p.705
Plenums, wiring in	300.22 p.144
Pliable raceway	362.2 p.220
PLTC cables	725.154 p.647
Plug cap, attachment	DEF 100 p.26
Plug fuse	240.51(A) p.96
Plug fuse, maximum voltage	240.50 p.96
Plug rating, motor-comp.	440.55(B) p.346
Plug, attachment cap	406.7 p.272
Plug, attachment	DEF 100 p.26
Plug, portable X-Ray	517.72(C) p.455
Plug, wooden not used in mounting	110.13(A) p.35
Plugging box	DEF 530.2 p.472
Plugging boxes, AC system	530.18(E) p.474
Plugging boxes, cords	530.18(E) p.474
Plugging boxes, lights	530.18(G) p.474
Plugging boxes, O.C.P.	530.18(E) p.474
Plugging boxes, receptacle	530.14 p.473
Plug-in device, busway	368.17(C) p.225
Plugmold raceways	Art. 384 p.235
Point of attachment	545.6 ex. p.477
Point of connection DC	250.164(A & B) p.128
Point of entrance	225.32 p.74
Point of entrance definition	800.2 p.670
Polarity of appliances	422.40 p.294
Polarity of connections	200.11 p.48
Polarity, thru bushed holes	230.54(E) p.84
Polarization of fixtures	410.50 p.283
Polarized attachment plugs	200.10(A&B) p.47
Polarized or grounding type plug	422.40 p.294
Polarized, adapter	406.10(B) p.273
Polarized, uniquely	604.6(C) p.526
Pole base	410.30(B1) p.282
Poles, climbing space	225.14(D) p.72
Poles, comm. cond spacing	800.133(A1) p.677
Poles, conductor separation	225.14(D) p.72
Poles, handhole	410.30(B1) p.282
Polyphase, transformer	450.3 p.348
Pool panelboard, insulated grd. cond.	680.25(B) p.583
Pool, bonding forming shells	680.26(B4) p.584
Pool, bonding metal parts	680.26(B7) p.584
Pool, conduit entries	680.24(D) p.583
Pool, cord length	680.7(A) p.577
Pool, cord strain relief	680.24(E) p.583
Pool, diving structures	680.26(B7) ex.#3 p.584
Pool, dry niche fixture	680.23(C) p.581
Pool, electrical covers	680.27(B) p.585
Pool, encapsulated termination	680.23(B2b) p.581
Pool, equipment room drainage	680.11 p.577
Pool, equipment to be grounded	680.24(F) p.583
Pool, fixture lens 18"	680.23(A5) p.580
Pool, fixture maximum voltage	680.23(A4) p.580
Pool, forming shell	680.23(B1) p.580
Pool, forming shell un-water sound	680.27(A)1 p.585
Pool, GFCI receptacles location	680.22(A4) p.580
Pool, grounding	680.6 p.577
Pool, grounding terminals	680.24(D) p.583
Pool, junction boxes	680.24(A) p.582
Pool, light fixture lens	680.23(A6) p.580
Pool, light fixtures location	680.22(B) p.579

Pool, lighting grd. conductor	680.23(F2) p.582	Potential difference	517.11 p.442
Pool, maximum fixture voltage	680.23(A4) p.580	Potential differences	517.19(C) *I.N.* p.444
Pool, maximum water level	680.2 Definitions p.576	Potential differences	250.60 *I.N. #2* p.113
Pool, normal water level	680.23(A5) p.580	Potential instrument transf., grounding	250.170 p.129
Pool, observation stands	680.26(B7) ex 3 p.584	Potential transformer protection	408.52 p. 277
Pool, overhead conductors	680.8 p.577	Potential transformer, fuses	450.3(C) p.348
Pool, paddle fan height	680.22(B1) p. 579	Potting compound, pool	680.23(B2b) p.581
Pool, panelboard grounding	680.24(F) p.583	Pound-inches, torque motor term.	430.9(C) p.314
Pool, potting compound	680.23(B2b) p.581	Powder coating	516.10(C) p.439
Pool, pump recpt.	680.22(A1) p.579	Power lines, switchboard	520.53(O) p.466
Pool, receptacles from wall	680.22(A1) p.579	Power and Control tray cable	336.2 p.199
Pool, recirculating pump recpt.	680.22(A1) p.579	Power conductors, spacing	225.14(D) p.72
Pool, steel tie wires	680.26(B1A) p.584	Power contacts, min.depth of oil	501.115(A1) p.383
Pool, storable definition	680.2 p.576	Power conversion equip.	430.124(A) p.333
Pool, storable GFCI	680.32 p.585	Power distribution blocks	314.28(E) p.183
Pool, switching devices	680.22(C) p.580	Power failure	225.38(A) p.75
Pool, therapeutic	680.60 p.589	Power fuses in parallel	490.21(B1) p.361
Pool, transformer	680.23(A2) p.580	Power houses	110.19 ex. p.37
Pool, underwater audio	680.27(A2) p.585	Power interruption, phase converter	455.22 p.357
Pool, underwater lights	680.23 p.580	Power limited exposed cable	760.53(A1) p.654
Pool, underwater luminaires	680.23 p.580	Power limited fire signaling	760.136(A) p.656
Pool, underwater speakers	680.27(A) p.585	Power loss hazard	240.4(A) p.89
Pool, wading definition	680.2 p.576	Power operable switch, feeder	225.38(A) p.75
Pool, water heaters	680.9 p.577	Power panelboard protection	408.36(B) p.276
Pool, wet-niche fixture	680.23(B) p.580	Power production equipment, Definition	705.2 p.632
Pool-assoc. motors, equip. grd. cond.	680.21(A5) p.579	Power service drop conductors	230.28 p.80
Pools, swimming	Art. 680 p.575	Power supply cord, mobile homes	550.10(B) p.482
Porcelain covers, boxes	314.41 p.185	Power-driven machine	670.2 p.572
Porcelain knobs, open conductors	225.12 p.72	Power-limited circuits	Art. 725 p.641
Porcelain lampholders	410.122 p.286	Power-limited same enclosure fire signal	760.136(A) p.656
Port. switchboards, cond. marking	520.53(H2) p.464	Power-limited tray cable	T.725.154(G) p.648
Portable appliance, 80% of circuit	210.23(A1) p.54	Pre-energization tests	225.56 p.76
Portable appliance, definition	550.2 p.481	Predetermined cells, raceway	374.2 p.229
Portable cables over 600v	400.30 p.261	Premises, laundry	Example D4a p.807
Portable equip., grd. electrode	250.188(E) p.131	Premises-powered broadband	Art. 840 p.707
Portable generators	250.34(A) p.110	Pressure connectors	110.14(A) p.36
Portable lamps	410.82 p.285	Pressure plates	424.59 *I.N.* p.300
Portable lamps, cords	400.7(A) p.260	Pressure plates, egress	110.26(C3) p.39
Portable lamps, spray area	516.4(D) p.437	Pressure-relief vent	450.25 p.353
Portable motor 1/3 hp	430.81(B) p.327	Pressurized sulfur hexafluoride gas	326.112 p.191
Portable outdoor signs GFCI	600.10(C2) p.522	Prevailing conditions, services	230.70(C) p.84
Portable power cable	T.400.4 p.253	Prevent energizing of the machine	501.125(A4) p.383
Portable power cable	T.400.4 p.253	Preventing pull on a cord	400.10 *I.N.* p.260
Portable signs,	600.10 p.521	Primary leads, ballast	300.3(C2b) p.136
Portable supply cable marking	520.53(H2) p.464	Prime mover	700.12(B1) p.625
Portable switch., interconnections	520.53(J) p.465	Prime mover, battery conductors	480.4 p.359
Portable switchboards, exhibition	518.5 p.459	Products of combustion	300.21 p.144
Portable switchboards, neutral	520.53(O) p.466	Projection ports	540.10 p.476
Portable tools wet location	250.114(4G) p.122	Projectors, incandescent-type	540.13 p.477
Positive mechanical ventilation	516.3(F) p.436	Prolonged submersion	T.110.28 p.41
Positive-pressure ventilat.	501.125 p.383	Prolonged submersion, motor	T.110.28 p.41
Potential coils switchboard	408.52 page 277	Prongs, blades, or pins attach. plug	406.7(D) p.272

Propagation of flame	501.15(E1) ex.2 p.380	Raceway, ENT pliable	Art. 362 p.220
Propagation of flames	501.15 *I.N. #2* p.377	Raceway, external joiners	T.384.22 *note p.236
Propane	500.6(A4) *I.N. #1* p.371	Raceway, internal joiners	T.384.22 †note p.236
Proper maintenance	90.1(B) p.22	Raceways arranged to drain, bldgs.	225.22 p.73
Propylene oxide	500.6(A)2 ex.2 p.371	Raceways arranged to drain, service	230.53 p.83
Proscenium lights, stage	520.41(A) p.462	Raceways, circular	310.15(B3c) p.152
Protect., conduct. & cables in tunnel	110.51(C) p.44	Raceways, complete system	300.18 p.143
Protection from foreign systems	110.26(E1b) p.39	Raceways, continuity	300.10 p.141
Protective covers, flat cable	322.112 p.188	Raceways, different temperatures	300.7 p.140
Protector grding electrode cond.	800.90(B) *I.N.* p.673	Raceways, end fitting into panel	408.5 p.275
Protector location	800.90(B) *I.N.* p.673	Raceways, flat-top	390.4(A) p.238
Psychiatric security rooms	517.18(B) ex.2 p.444	Raceways, half-round	390.4(A) p.238
Public address, sound	640.1 p.554	Raceways, induced currents	300.20(A) p.144
Pull and junction boxes	314.28 p.183	Raceways, installed complete	300.18 p.143
Pull point	300.15(A) p.142	Raceways, listed fixtures	410.64 p.285
Pump, dispensing disconnect	514.11(A) p.428	Raceways, means of support	300.11(B) p.141
Pumps, canned	501.17(F3) p.380	Raceways, on exterior surfaces	225.22 p.73
Pumps, fountain	680.50 p.588	Raceways, optical fiber	90.2(A) p.22
Pumps, submersible	501.140(A3) p.385	Raceways, other systems	300.8 p.140
Purpose is evident	110.22 p.37	Raceways, sealing	300.7(A) p.140
PVC conduit, expansion joints	352.44 p.210	Raceways, securing	300.11(A) p.141
PVC conduit, exposed	352.10(F) p.209	Raceways, short sections	300.18(A) ex. p.143
PVC conduit, joints	352.48 p.210	Raceways, spacing between	310.15(B3) p.150
PVC conduit, number of bends	352.26 p.209	Raceways, trench-type	390.3(C) p.238
PVC conduit, number of conductors	352.22 p.209	Racked, conductors	110.74 p.45
PVC conduit, splices & taps	352.56 p.210	Racks, open-conductors	225.12 p.72
PVC conduit, support	352.30(B) p.209	Radiant heating panels	424.90 p.302
PVC conduit, support of fixtures	352.12(B) p.209	Radiation or conduction, spray area	516.4(C5) p.437
PVC conduit, trimming	352.28 p.209	Radii of bends, flexing use	360.24(A) p.220
PVC rigid conduit	Art. 352 p.208	Radio & Television antennas	225.19(B) p.73
PVC thermal expansion,	T.352.44 p.210	Radio & Television equipment	Art. 810 p.682
		Radio-frequency converters	665.2 p.567
		Radiographic, X-ray	660.23(A) p.566

-Q-

		Radius of bends, armored cable	320.24 p.187
Quadruplex receptacles	517.19(B2) p.444	Radius of bends, conductors	110.3(A3) p.34
Qualified person	DEF 100 p.31	Radius of bends, conduit	Table 2 Chapt.9 p.711
Qualified personnel	520.53(P) p.466	Radius of bends, flex. metal	T.360.24 p.220
Qualified personnel	690.13 *I.N.* p.599	Radius of bends, gas cable	T.326.24 p.191
Qualified persons, isolating switch	230.204(C) p.88	Radius of bends, hi-voltage cable	300.34 p.145
Qualified testing laboratories	300.21 *I.N.* p.144	Radius of bends, lead-covered	300.34 p.145
		Radius of bends, metal clad cable	330.24 p.193
		Radius of bends, MI cable	332.24 p.195
		Radius of bends, nonshielded cable	300.34 p.145
		Radius of bends, romex	334.24 p.197
		Radius of bends, shielded cable	300.34 p.145

-R-

		Radius of the curve	Table 2 Chapt. 9 p.711
		Rail serving as conductor	610.21(F4) p.530
		Rails, clearance over	T.225.60 p.77
Raceway supported enclosure	314.23(F) p.181	Railway conductors	110.19 p.37
Raceway to open wiring	300.16 p.142	Rain, snow, sleet motor enclosure	T.110.28 p.41
Raceway seal, underground raceway	225.27 p.74	Rainproof	300.6(A2) p.140
Raceway transitions, direct burial	300.5(J) p.139	Raintight	300.6(A2) p.140

Entry	Reference
Raintight service head	230.54(A) p.83
Raised cover, receptacle 2 screws	406.5(C) p.271
Raised floor, computer	645.5(E) p.561
Range hoods, cord	422.16(B4) p. 293
Range, 1 ø on 3 ø system	220.55 p.65
Range, disconnect	422.33(B) p.293
Range, dryer cable	T.400.4 p.256
Range, equip. grd. conductor-neutral	400.5(B) p.258
Range, feeder demand	T.220.55 p.66
Range, grounded conductor	250.140 p.126
Range, neutral 70%	220.61(B1) p.67
Range, taps	210.19(A3) ex.1 p.53
Rate schedules	230.2(D) p.79
Rated input to power conversion	430.122(A) p.333
Rated over 300va	422.31(B) p. 293
Rated-load current	440.6(A) ex.1 p.341
Rated-load current A/C	440.2 p.340
Ratings in volts & amps	424.29 p.298
Ratings in volts & watts	424.29 p.298
Reactor, space separation	470.3 p.359
Reactors, combustible materials	470.18(C) p.359
Reactors, metallic enclosures	470.18(E) p.359
Reactors, temperature rise	470.18(E) p.359
Readily accessible disconnect, A/C	440.14 p. 343
Readily accessible, motor switch	430.107 p.331
Readily accessible, O.C.P.	240.24(A) p.95
Readily accessible, switches	404.8(A) p.267
Readily distinguishable solid color	400.22(A) p.261
Readily identified, emerg. systems	700.10(A) p.623
Readily ignitible residues	516.10(C1) ex. p.439
Reamed, rigid conduit	344.28 p.204
Reasonable eff.,volt. drop	210.19(A) I.N. #4 p.53
Re-bar electrodes	250.52(A3) p.112
Rec. vehicles, interior wiring	551.40(B) p.493
Receiving sta. outdoor antenna	T.810.16(A) p.683
Receptacle loads, demand factor	T.220.44 p.66
Receptacle outlet cord pendant	210.50(A) p.55
Receptacle rating, motor-comp.	440.55(B) p.346
Receptacle, 15a on 20a circuit	T.210.21(B2) p.54
Receptacle, AC	210.63 p. 58
Receptacle, adjacent to basin	210.52(D) p.57
Receptacle, basement	210.52(G) p.58
Receptacle, bathroom	210.52(D) p.57
Receptacle, bonding at box	250.146 p.127
Receptacle, circuit rating	T.210.21(B3) p.54
Receptacle, counter top space	210.52(C) p.56
Receptacle, floor	210.52(A3) p.56
Receptacle, garage	210.52(G) p.58
Receptacle, hallway	210.52(H) p.58
Receptacle, heat-AC	210.63 p.58
Receptacle, individual b.c.	210.21(B1) p.54
Receptacle, laundry	210.52(F) p.57
Receptacle, malfunctioning	555.19(A) I.N. p.515
Receptacle, maximum load	T.210.21(B2) p. 54
Receptacle, nongrounding type	406.4(D2) p.271
Receptacle, not attended	406.9(B2)(a) p.273
Receptacle, outdoors	210.52(E) p.57
Receptacle, overheating	555.19 I.N. p.515
Receptacle, pilot light	520.73 p.468
Receptacle, rating	T.210.21(B3) p.54
Receptacle, refrigerator	210.52(B1) ex. 2 p.56
Receptacle, replacement	406.4(D) p.271
Receptacle, rooftop	210.63 p.58
Receptacle, single	210.21(B1) p.54
Receptacle, technical power systems	647.7(A2) p.564
Receptacle, T-slot	406.8 p.273
Receptacle, yoke	DEF 100 p.31
Receptacles	Art. 406 p.270
Receptacles, AC or DC	406.4(F) p.271
Receptacles, anesthetizing loc.	517.61(B5) p.453
Receptacles, attachment plugs	406.7 p.272
Receptacles, bar-type counters	210.52(A2)(3) p.56
Receptacles, behind door	210.52(A2)(1) p.56
Receptacles, cleat-type	410.5 ex. p.280
Receptacles, clock	210.52(B2) ex.1 p.56
Receptacles, CO/ALR	406.3(C) p.270
Receptacles, construction sites	590.4(D)(1) p.517
Receptacles, counter top space	210.52(C) p.56
Receptacles, critical care area	517.19(B) p.444
Receptacles, damp location	406.9(A) p.272
Receptacles, demand factor 10kva	220.44 p.64
Receptacles, demand shore power	T.555.12 p.514
Receptacles, different frequencies	406.4(F) p.271
Receptacles, dressing rooms	520.73 p.468
Receptacles, dwelling spacing	210.52 p.55
Receptacles, dwelling spacing	550.13(D) p.485
Receptacles, exemption GFCI	210.8(A) ex.2 p.50
Receptacles, faceplates	406.6 p.272
Receptacles, face-up position	406.5(E) p.272
Receptacles, fixed panels, planters	210.52(A2)(2) p.56
Receptacles, floor protection	406.9(D) p.273
Receptacles, free standing counters	210.52(A2)(3) p.56
Receptacles, frequencies	406.4(F) p.271
Receptacles, gas-fired ranges	210.52(B2) ex.2 p.56
Receptacles, general care area	517.18(B) p.444
Receptacles, grounding poles	406.10 p.273
Receptacles, grounding type	406.4(D1) p.271
Receptacles, grounding type	410.59(B) p.284
Receptacles, guest rooms	210.60 p.58
Receptacles, height dwelling	210.52 p.55
Receptacles, hospital grade	517.18(B) p.444
Receptacles, hotels/motels	210.60 p.58
Receptacles, ignition system	210.52(B2) ex.2 p.56
Receptacles, island counter top	210.52(C2) p.56

Receptacles, isolated ground	406.3(D) p.270
Receptacles, kitchen counter	210.52(C) p.56
Receptacles, location 5 1/2'	210.52 p.55
Receptacles, locking & grd. type	555.19(A) p.515
Receptacles, marinas	555.19 p.515
Receptacles, mobile home spacing	550.13 p.484
Receptacles, multiwire	210.4(B) p.48
Receptacles, no limit dwelling	220.14(J) p.63
Receptacles, nongrounding type	406.4(D2) p.271
Receptacles, office furnishings	605.5(C) p.526
Receptacles, orange triangle	406.3(D) p.270
Receptacles, outdoor balconies	210.52(E3) p.57
Receptacles, outdoors dwelling	210.52(E) p.57
Receptacles, ovens	210.52(B2) ex.2 p.56
Receptacles, patient bed	517.18(B) p.444
Receptacles, pediatric locations	517.18(C) p.444
Receptacles, peninsular counter top	210.52(C3) p.56
Receptacles, pigtail	300.13(B) p.141
Receptacles, plugging boxes	530.14 p.473
Receptacles, pool	680.22 p.579
Receptacles, pool GFCI	680.22(A4) p.579
Receptacles, portable cords	406.4(E) p.271
Receptacles, protect from weather	406.9 p.272
Receptacles, quadruplex	517.19(B2) p.444
Receptacles, railings	210.52(A2)(3) p.56
Receptacles, raised cover 2 screws	406.5(C) p.271
Receptacles, required dwelling	210.52 p.55
Receptacles, room dividers	210.52(A2)(3) p.56
Receptacles, shore power	555.19(A) p.515
Receptacles, show window 12'	210.62 p.58
Receptacles, showcases	410.59(C) p.284
Receptacles, sliding panels	210.52(A2)(2) p.56
Receptacles, spa or hot tub	680.40 p.586
Receptacles, stage	520.45 p.463
Receptacles, tamper resistant	517.18(C) p.444
Receptacles, water accumulation	406.9 p.272
Receptacles, wet location	406.9(B) p.272
Receptacles. rec. vehicle	551.41 p.493
Recepts., baseboard heater	210.52(A) *I.N.* p.56
Recepts., baseboard heaters	424.9 *I.N.* p. 296
Recepts., flush mount faceplate	406.9(E) p. 273
Recepts., weatherproof faceplate	406.9(E) p.273
Recessed fixture clearance Type IC	410.116(A2) p.286
Recessed fluorescent fixture	410.16(A2) p.281
Recessed incandescent fixture	410.16(A1) p.281
Recessed incandescent fixtures	410.16(C3) p.281
Recessed incandescent, thermal prot.	410.115(C) p.286
Reciprocators, spray application	516.10(A2) p.438
Recording equipment	640.1 p.554
Recreational vehicle sites, 30a recept.	551.71 p.500
Recreational vehicles, appl.	551.2 *I.N.* p.490
Recreational vehicles, auto trans.	551.20(E) p.492
Recreational vehicles, frame	551.2 p.490
Recreational vehicles, GFCI	551.41(C) p.493
Recreational vehicles, panelboard	551.45 p.495
Recreational vehicles, parks	551.2 Def. p.490
Recreational vehicles, tent sites	551.73(A) p.501
Rectifier bridge, motors	430.22(A1) p.316
Rectifier voltage, motors	430.18 p.316
Rectifier, ground	250.162 ex.2 p.128
Rectifier, grounding organ	650.5 p.564
Rectifier, transformer-type organ	650.4 p.564
Reducing objectionable noise	647.3 p.563
Reflecting systems, solar	690.53 *I.N.* p.605
Refrigerating equipment	440.1 p.340
Refrigerator, receptacle	210.52(B1)ex. 2 p.56
Refrigerators, rec. vehicle	551.2 *I.N.* p.490
Regenerated energy, elevators	620.91(A) p.543
Relays, motor overload	430.40 p.321
Release-type adhesive, FCC cable	324.41 p.190
Relocatable partitions, outlets	605.8(C) p.527
Relocate wired partitions, cord & plug	605.5(B) p.526
Remote control signal circuits, safety	725.31 p.642
Remote crane controls, cell line	668.32(B) p.571
Remote disconnect, water pump	230.72(A) ex. p.85
Remote hoist controls, cell line	668.32(B) p.571
Remote-control circuits	Art. 725 p.641
Remote-control conductors	430.72(B) p.326
Removable truck panels, feeder	225.51 ex. p.76
Removal of a drawer, ranges	422.33(B) p.293
Removed from the raceway, outlets	374.7 p.229
Removed from the raceway, outlets	390.7 p.239
Repairing drywall no gaps 1/8"	314.21 p.180
Replaceable in the field	422.61 p. 295
Replaceable in the field	424.29 p.298
Reproduction equipment	640 p.554
Reproduction, sound	640.1 p.554
Residual voltage capacitor	460.6(A) p.357
Residues	516.4(B) p.436
Resist.-type heating appliances	422.11(F) p.291
Resistance elements, heat	424.22(B) p.297
Resistance of conductors, AC	Table 9 p.722
Resistance of conductors, DC	Table 8 p.721
Resistance of made electrodes	250.53(2) ex. p.112
Resistance welder	630.31 p.553
Resistance, AC	Table 9 p.722
Resistance, DC	Table 8 p.721
Resistance, ground rod 25 ohm	250.53(2) ex. p.112
Resistance-type boilers	424.70 p.300
Resistant to crushing, PVC	352.100 p.210
Resistant to distortion, PVC	352.100 p.210
Resistivity, thermal	310.2 DEF p.147
Resistor duty, motors	T.430.23(C) p.317
Resistors and Reactors	Art. 470 p.358

Resistors, combustible materials	470.18(C) p.359
Resistors, space separation	470.3 p.359
Restaurant, place of assembly	518.2(A) p.458
Restrict the sizing	110.14(C2) *I.N.* p.36
Restricted access circuit breakers	240.6(C) p.91
Rheostats, motor-starting	430.82(C) p.328
Ribbon cable	522.21(B) p.469
Ride device	522.2DEF p.468
Right angles to the cells	372.5 p.228
Rigid conduit, bends	Table 2 Chap. 9 p.711
Rigid conduit, buried	Table 300.5 p.138
Rigid conduit, durably identified	344.120 p.205
Rigid conduit, reamed	344.28 p.204
Rigid conduit, standard length	344.130 p.205
Rigid conduit, supports	344.30(B) p.204
Rigid conduit, threadless connectors	344.42(A) p.205
Rigid metal conduit corrosion	344.10(B) p.204
Rigid metal conduit stem	501.130(A3) p.384
Rigid metal conduit, size	344.20 p.204
Rigid NMC, expansion joints	352.44 p.210
Rigid nonmetallic conduit	Art. 352 p.208
Rigid nonmetallic conduit bodies	352.10(H) p.209
Rigid nonmetallic conduit, install.	352.10 p.208
Rigid nonmetallic conduit, not permit.	352.12 p.209
Rigid polyvinyl chloride conduit	Art. 352 p.208
Rigid structural system, cable tray	392.2 p.239
Ring, box extension	314.22 p.180
Risk assessment	708.4 p.636
Risk of ignition	501.125(B) *I.N.* #2 p.384
Rivets, screws, bolts fasten lights	410.36(B) p.282
RMC threadless couplings	344.42(A) p.205
RMS open-circuit voltage	410.151(C8) p.289
RMS, voltage definition	Art. 100 p.33
Road show connection, theaters	520.50 p.463
Robot, arm	516.10(A) p.438
Robotic, devices	516.10(A) p.438
Robotic, programing	516.10(A) p.438
Rock bottom, ground rod	250.53(G) p.113
Rod and pipe electrodes	250.52(A5) p.112
Rolling stock	90.2(B1) p.22
Romex, ampacity	334.80 p.198
Romex, attic joists	334.23 p.197
Romex, bends in cable	334.24 p.197
Romex, fished in air voids	334.10(A2) p.196
Romex, fished NM box	334.30 p.197
Romex, in cement blocks	334.10(A2) p.196
Romex, in dropped or suspend. ceil.	334.12(A2) p.196
Romex, in raceway grounding	250.86 ex.1 p.117
Romex, installed in a raceway	362.22 p.221
Romex, installed in a raceway	342.22 p.202
Romex, knockout opening	314.17(C) ex. p.180
Romex, pool pump	680.21(A4) p.579
Romex, protection from damage	334.15(B) p.197
Romex, sizes #14 - #2	334.104 p.198
Romex, supports	334.30 p.197
Romex, temporary wiring	590.4(B & C) p.517
Romex, under one cable clamp	110.3(B) p.35
Romex, uses	334.10 p.196
Roof required over equipment	110.11 p.35
Roof/ceiling assembly	300.11(A1) p.141
Rooftop outlet	210.63 p.58
Rooftop receptacle	210.63 p.58
Room air conditioners, cords	440.64 p.346
Rooms for bulk chemicals	300.6(D) *I.N.* p.140
Rooms for casings	300.6(D) *I.N.* p.140
Rooms for fertilizer	300.6(D) *I.N.* p.140
Rooms for hides	300.6(D) *I.N.* p.140
Rooms for salt	300.6(D) *I.N.* p.140
Root-mean-square current	620.13 *I.N.* p.535
Root-mean-square, voltage	DEF 100 p.33
Ropes, chains or sticks busways	368.17(C) p.225
Rostrums	513.7(E) p.423
Rotary, phase converter	455.2 DEF p.355
Round access opening, manhole	110.75 p.45
Round boxes	314.2 p.177
RTRC conduit	355.1 p.213
RTRC maximum size	355.20(B) p.214
Rubber mats, motors	430.233 p.335
Rubber mats, switchboards	250.174(C) p.129
Rubber-filled cords	T.400.4 note 5 p.257
Rules, permissive	90.5(B) p.24
Rung spacing, ladder cable tray	392.10(B1a) p.240
Running boards	398.15(C2) p.249
Running boards, AC cable	320.23(B) p.186
Running overload prot. shunted	430.35(A&B) p.320
Running threads conduit	344.42(B) p.205
RV site, grounding conductor	551.76(A) p.501

-S-

S loops direct burial	300.5(J) *I.N.* p.139
S type fuse	240.53 p.96
Safeguarding of persons & property	90.1(A) p.22
Safety control equip. remote control	725.31(A) p.642
SCADA	708.2DEF p.636
Scatter box DEF	530.2 p.472
Scatter of cell parts, batteries	480.10(B) p.360
Scene docks, back stage lamps	520.47 p.463
Scenery, bracket wiring	520.63(A) p.466
Schedule 80 PVC conduit	300.5(D4) p.139
Schedule 80 PVC conduit	Art. 352 p.208
Screw shell, fuseholder	240.50(E) p.96

Screw shell, lampholder	410.50 p.283	Service equipment marking	230.66 p.84
Screw shells	200.10(C) p.48	Service factor, motors	430.32(A1) p.319
Screwed on, boxes	110.31(D) p.42	Service fuses	230.90(A) ex.2 p.86
Screwshell luminaires	647.8(C) p.564	Service head, attachment point	230.54(C) p.83
Scuttle hole	320.23(A) p.186	Service head, wet location	230.54(A) p.83
SE cable, interior wiring	338.10(B4a) p.200	Service lateral,	DEF 100 p.32
SE cable, temperature limitations	338.10(B3) p.200	Service lateral, minimum size	230.31(B) ex. p.81
Seal unused knock outs	110.12(A) p.35	Service mast	230.28 p.80
Sealed batteries, prevent scatter	480.10(B) p.360	Service point	DEF 100 p.32
Sealing 2" conduit Class I Div.1	501.15(A1) p.377	Service size minimum 60 amp	230.79(D) p.85
Sealing against dampness	324.40 p.189	Service, bonding	250.92(B) p.117
Sealing compound	501.15 p.377	Service, disconnect location	230.70(A1) p.84
Sealing compound, thickness	501.15(C3) p.379	Service, floating dock	555.12 p.513
Sealing of strands	501.15 p.377	Service, gooseneck	230.54(B) p.83
Sealing raceways	300.7(A) p.140	Service, liquidtight flexible conduit	230.43(16) p.82
Seals, Class I, Div.1	501.15(A) p.377	Service, prevailing conditions	230.70(C) p.84
Seals, Class I, Div.2	501.15(B2) p.378	Service, raceway seal	230.8 p.79
Seashore areas	300.6(D) I.N. p.140	Service, THHN conductors	T.310.104(A) p.169
Second ground fault	517.19(F) I.N. p.445	Service, THHN conductors	310.10(B) p.148
Secondary circuits, wound-rotor	430.23 p.317	Service-drop attachment 24"	230.54(C) ex. p.83
Secondary ties, O.C.P.	450.6(B) p.351	Service-ent. cables, protection	230.50(A) p.82
Selected receptacles, definition	517.2 p.442	Service-entrance cable definition	338.2 p.200
Selective coordination	DEF 100 p.27	Service-entrance cables, supports	230.51(A) p.83
Self-excited	705.40 I.N. #2 p.634	Service-entrance capped elbows	314.16(C3) p.179
Self-propelled machinery	90.2(B2) p.22	Service-entrance cond. 600v O.C.P.	230.208(B) p.88
Self-propelled vehicles	511.1 p.419	Service-lateral cond., minimum	230.31(B) p.81
Self-restoring ground. contact	250.138(A) ex. p.126	Service-Lateral conductors, spliced	230.33 p.81
Self-service stations	514.11(C) p.429	Services over 35,000 volts	230.212 p.88
Sense motor rotation	430.35(B1) p.321	Services, alum. neutral undergrd.	230.30 ex.4 p.81
Sensitive electronic equipment	647.1 p.563	Services, clearances from bldgs.	230.9 p.79
Sensors, occupancy	210.70(A) ex.2 p.58	Services, clearances from ground	230.24(B) p.80
Sep.derived syst.,metal water pipe	250.104(A3) p.119	Services, connections to terminals	230.81 p.85
Separable locking-type connectors	410.59 p.284	Services, continuous load	230.42(A1) p.82
Separate building, grounding	250.32(D) p.110	Services, disconnect	230.70 p.84
Separate compartments, raceways	386.70 p.237	Services, disconnect GFCI	230.95 I.N. #3 p.87
Separate services same electrode	250.58 p.113	Services, disconnect max. number	230.71(A) p.84
Separately bushed openings	230.54(E) p.84	Services, disconnect neutral	230.75 p.85
Separately derived 6-phase wye	647.5 p.563	Services, disconnect simultaneously	230.74 p.85
Separately derived syst. grd. elect.	250.30(A4) p.107	Services, drip loops	230.54(F) p.84
Separately derived system	DEF 100 p.31	Services, drop point of attachment	230.26 p.80
Separately derived systems	250.30 p.106	Services, electrical bonding	250.92(A) p.117
Separation between showcases	410.59(C)(2) p.284	Services, emergency supply	230.94 ex.4 p.86
Sequential delayed	517.34(A) ex. p.449	Services, fire pump & equip.	230.94 ex.4 p.86
Serious degradation	310.15(A3) p.149	Services, floating buildings	553.5 p.512
Service cables support	230.51(A) p.83	Services, GFCI solid-wye 1000a	230.95 p.87
Service cond., manuf. build.	545.6 ex. p.477	Services, grounding conductor size	T.250.122 p.125
Service conductors, cable tray support	230.44 p.82	Services, group disconnects	230.72 p.85
Service conductors, fire pump	695.3(A1) p.616	Services, handle ties	230.71(B) p.84
Service conductors, spliced	230.46 p.82	Services, head point of attach.	230.54(C) ex. p.83
Service disconnect, bathrooms	230.70(A2) p.84	Services, heights vertical	230.24(B) p.80
Service equip., marking	550.32(G) p.490	Services, high-voltage	230.200 p.87
Service equipment illumination	110.26(D) p.39	Services, indicate open or closed	230.77 p.85

Services, insulation or covered	230.22 p.79	Short-circuit current available	230.205(B) p.88
Services, load management	230.94 ex.3 p.86	Short-time duty, motors	T.430.22(E) p.317
Services, locked O.C.P.	230.92 p.86	Show window light., feeder 200va	220.14(G) p.62
Services, lugs not solder	230.81 p.85	Show window receptacles 12'	210.62 p.58
Services, masts as supports	230.28 p.80	Showcases, cord support	410.59(C) p.284
Services, means of attachment	230.27 p.80	Showcases, female fitting	410.59(C)(3) p.284
Services, mechanical strength	230.23(A) p.79	Showcases, free lead at the end	410.59(C)(3) p.284
Services, minimum conductor size	230.202(A) p.87	Showcases, receptacles	410.59(B) p.284
Services, minimum size 60 amp	230.79(D) p.85	Shunting means, cell line	668.14 p.570
Services, mobile homes	550.30 p.489	Shunting, motors	430.35 p.320
Services, neutral size minimum	230.42(C) p. 82	Shunting, service	230.94 ex.2 p.86
Services, neutral size overhead	230.23(C) p. 80	SI units	Annex D examples p.804
Services, number allowed	230.2 p.78	Side of a building	225.19 ex.4 p.73
Services, other conductors	230.7 p.79	Sidewalks, excavating	314.29 p.184
Services, outside a bldg.	230.6 p.79	Sidewalks, moving	620.1 p.532
Services, over 600v minimum size	230.202(A) p.87	Sign & outline lighting load	220.14(F) p.62
Services, over top of window	230.9 ex. p.79	Sign, aluminum thickness	600.8(C) p.521
Services, pressure connectors	230.81 p.85	Sign, GFCI location	600.10(C2) p.522
Services, rating of disconnect	230.79 p85	Sign, vehicles height	600.9(A) p.521
Services, shore power	555.12 p.513	Signal circuits, traveling cable	620.12(A) p.535
Services, short-circuit current avail.	110.10 p.35	Signal processing, audio	Art. 640 p.554
Services, simultaneously disconnect	230.74 p.85	Signal, heated appliance	422.42 p.294
Services, six operations of hand	230.71(B) p.84	Signaling circuits	Art. 725 p.641
Services, size and rating	230.42(B) p.82	Signals, derangement	700.6(A) p.623
Services, spliced	230.46 p.82	Significant capacitance	705.40 *I.N. #2* p.634
Services, surge arresters	230.82(4) p.86	Sign-outline lighting enclosure	300.3(C2a) p.136
Services, taps to main	230.46 p.82	Signs	Art. 600 p.519
Services, top of window	230.9 ex. p.79	Signs, ballasts	600.21 p.522
Services, undergrd. wiring meth	230.50(A) p.82	Signs, accessible to pedestrians	600.5(A) p.519
Services, underground lateral	230.30 p.81	Signs, branch circuit rating	600.5(B1) p.519
Services, vertical clearances	230.24(B) p.80	Signs, breaker in sight of	600.6(A)(1) p.520
Severe corrosive influences IMC	342.10(B) p.202	Signs, computed load	220.14(F) p.62
Severe deterioration	110.11 *I.N. #2* p.35	Signs, cutouts-flashers	600.6(B) p.520
Severe over-voltage	705.40 *I.N. #2* p.634	Signs, disconnect	600.6 p.520
Sewerage disposal	701.2 *I.N.* p.627	Signs, drain holes	600.9(D1) p.521
Shaded-pole motor	430.6(A1) ex.2 p.312	Signs, electromech. control	600.6(A2) p.520
Shaft seals compressor	440.2 p.340	Signs, elevation above vehicles	600.9(A) p.521
Sharply angular substance, backfill	300.5(F) p.139	Signs, enclosure wood	600.9(C) p.521
Sheet-metal screws	250.8(A) p.103	Signs, exposed to weather	600.9(D) p.521
Sheet-metal troughs, wireways	376.2 p.230	Signs, flashers-cutouts	600.6(B) p.520
Shield system, FCC cable	324.40(C) p.190	Signs, gas tube cord length	600.10(D2) p.522
Shielded, cables over 600v	400.32 p.261	Signs, listed	600.3 p.519
Shielded, fuses or breakers	240.41(A) p.96	Signs, location	600.9 p.521
Shielding, conductors	310.10(E) p.148	Signs, marking	600.4 p.519
Shields shall be grounded	504.50(B) p.396	Signs, material	600.8(B) p.521
Shields, cables over 600v	400.32 p.261	Signs, neon tubing	600.41 p.524
Shock hazard during relamp	680.23(A3) p.580	Signs, outdoor portable GFCI	600.10(C2) p.522
Shore power, receptacles	555.19(A) p.515	Signs, outlet required	600.5(A) p.519
Short circuits, free from	110.7 p.35	Signs, over 600v transformers	600.23 p.522
Short radius capped elbows	314.16(C3) p.179	Signs, skeleton-type	600.30 p.523
Short radius conduit bodies	314.16(C3) p.179	Signs, supply leads enclosed	600.8 p.521
Short sections of raceway	300.12 ex. (1) p.141	Signs, tube support	600.41(B) p.524

Signs, tubing	600.41 p.524	Soft-drawn copper, antenna	810.11 ex. p.682
Signs, wood decoration	600.9(C) p.521	Solar cell, definition	690.2 p.595
Sill height, transformer	450.43(B) p.354	Solar photovoltaic systems	690 p.593
Simple react. ballast, therm. protect	410.130(E2) p.287	Solar system, ampacity	690.8(B) p.598
Simple reactance ballasts	410.130(E2) p.287	Solar system, O.C.P.	690.9(A) p.598
Simulating lightning, theaters	520.66 p.467	Solar, disconnect	690.13 p.599
Simultaneously disconnect feeder	225.38(B) p.75	Solar, neutral ampacity	705.95 p.635
Simultaneously, disconnect	210.4(B) p.48	Solar, storage batteries	690.71 p.605
Simultaneously, disconnect	230.74 p.85	Solar, unbalanced interconnect.	705.100 p.635
Simultaneously, disconnect lamph.	410.93 p.285	Solder, depend upon	230.81 p.85
Single branch circuit, feeder	225.39(A) p.75	Soldered splices joined mechanical	110.14(B) p.36
Single conductor, ampacities	394.104 p.247	Solely by enamel, boxes	314.40(A) *I.N.* p. 184
Single conductor, ferromagnetic	427.47 p. 309	Solely by enamel, EMT protection	358.12(2) p.218
Single conductors, installation	300.3(A) p. 135	Solid dielectric insulated conductors	310.10(E) p.148
Single enclosure, limit circuits	90.8(B) p.24	Solidly grounded	250.1 p.100
Single machine, A/C system	440.8 p.341	Solidly grounded neutral	230.95 p.87
Single pole breakers with handle ties	240.15(B4) p.92	Solidly grounded neutral	250.184 p.129
Single pole, insulated conductor	200.7(C1) p.47	Solid-state devices & tubes	665.2 p.567
Single screw on covers	406.5(C) p.271	Sound recording, cord size	640.42 p.559
Single-pole separable connectors	520.53(K) p.465	Sound-record, wireways-gut.	640.24 p.558
Single-pole separable connectors	530.22 p.475	Sound-recording	640.1 p.554
Sink, wet bar	210.8(A7) p.50	Sources of heat, discharge lamps	410.104(A) p.286
Six operations of the hand, feeder	225.33(B) p.75	Space heating, branch circuit	424.3(A) p.296
Six-cycle separation	708.52(D) p.640	Space heating, feeder	220.51 p.64
Skating rink	518.2(A) p.458	Space separation, resistors	470.3 p.359
Skeleton-type, signs	600.30 p.523	Spaces, public	210.8(B4) p. 51
Skin effect heating	426.40 p.306	Spacing bare metal parts	T.408.5 p.275
Skin effect heating definition	426.2 p.307	Spacing between conduits	310.15(3)(5b) p.152
Slash rating circuit breaker	240.85 p.97	Spacing bus bars motors	430.97(D) p.329
Sliding panels receptacle spacing	210.52(A2) p.56	Spacing for conductor supports	T.300.19(A) p.143
Slip rings	522.20 p.469	Spark gap, surge arrester	280.24(B) p.132
Small appl. circuits, no other outlets	210.52(B2) p.56	Sparks, open motors	430.14(B) p.316
Small appliance branch circuits	210.11(C1) p. 52	Spa-hot tub, paddle fan height	680.43(B1) p. 587
Small appliance, feeder load 1500va	220.52(A) p.65	Spa-hot tub, water heaters	680.9 p.577
Small appliance, no other outlets	210.52(B2) p.56	Spas & hot tubs	680.40 p.586
Small appliances 20 amp	210.52(B) p.56	Spas, GFCI	680.43(A2) p.587
Small conductors as taps	240.4(D) p.90	SPD, surge-protective devices	Art. 285 p.133
Small motor compressors	440.12(C) p.342	Speakers, underwater pool	680.27(A1) p.585
Small wind electric systems	Art. 694 p.610	Special effects, stage	520.66 p.467
Smoke generation, ENT	362.100 p.222	Special permission from inspector	90.2(C) p.23
Smoke removal systems	701.2 *I.N.* p.627	Special permission, conductor size	372.10 p.228
Smoothing iron stand	422.45 p.294	Specification, design	90.1(C) p.22
Smoothing irons 50 watts	422.43(A) p.294	Speech-input systems, sound	640.1 p.554
Snap switch as disconnect	225.36 ex. p.75	Spiders	530.15(D) p.473
Snap switch CO/ALR	404.14(C) p.269	Splice or tap loop wiring	390.7 p.239
Snap switch faceplates, grounding	404.9(B) p.268	Splices & taps, antennas	810.14 p.683
Snap switches, ganged 300v	404.8(B) p.268	Splices & taps, boxes	352.56 p.210
Snap switches, grounding	404.9(B) p.268	Splices & taps, buried cables	300.5(E) p.139
Snapswitch disc. means, feeder	225.36 ex p.75	Splices & taps, conduit bodies	314.16(C2) p.178
Snow melt. embedded in masonry	426.20(C2) p.305	Splices & taps, cords	400.9 p.260
Snow-melting equip. GFP	426.28 p.306	Splices & taps, gutters	366.56 p.223
Snow-melting equipment	Art. 426 p.304	Splices & taps, headers	374.6 p.229

Entry	Reference
Splices & taps, raceway	300.13(A) p.141
Splices & taps, services	230.46 p.82
Splices & taps, wireways	378.56 p.232
Splices equivalent to	110.14(B) p.36
Splices in cables, shielding	300.50(D) p.147
Splices, embedded cables	424.40 p.299
Splices, ground. elect. conductor	250.64(C) p.114
Splices, require box	300.15(A) p.142
Splicing device, not twisted together	110.14(B) p.36
Spotlight ports, projection from	540.10 p.476
Spray application pits	516.3(B6) p.434
Spray area, portable lamps	516.4(D) p.437
Spray booth	516.2 p.434
Spread of Fire	300.21 p.144
Spreaders, cables in concrete	424.44(C) p.300
Sprinkler prot., dedicated space	110.26(E1c) p.39
Stables, corrosive condition	300.6(D) I.N. p.140
Stage cables, studios 400%	530.18(A) p.474
Stage lighting, demand factor	T.530.19(A) p.474
Stage lights, branch circuit 20 amp	520.41 p.462
Stage lights, conduct. insulation	520.42 p.462
Stage pockets for receptacles	520.46 p.463
Stage set lighting cables 400%	530.18(A) p.474
Stage set lighting, B.C. receptacles	520.9 p.460
Stage smoke detectors, ventilators	520.49 p.463
Stage switchboard, metal hood	520.24 p.461
Stage, border lights	520.41 p.462
Stage, footlights	520.41 p.462
Stage, proscenium lights	520.41 p.462
Stage, receptacles	520.45 p.463
Stainless steel ground rods	250.52(A5b) p.112
Stairs, clearance	230.9(A) p.79
Stairway chair lifts	620.1 p.532
Stairways, permanent	110.33(B) p.42
Stanchions, aircraft hangars	513.7(E) p.423
Stand-alone system definition	690.2 p.595
Stand-alone system	692.2 p.607
Standard classification branch circuit	210.3 p.48
Standard lampholders, not less than 660w	720.5 p.640
Standard size overcurrent protection	240.6 p.91
Stand-by currents	665.10(A) p.567
Standby power, 60 seconds	701.12 p.628
Standby systems, battery	701.12(A) p.629
Standby systems, generator	701.12(B) p.629
Standpipes, floor receptacles	406.9(D) p.273
Standstill, oper. torque motors	430.7(C) p.313
Starting torque, modify	455.2 I.N. p.355
Starting current of motor	430.52(B) p.322
Static and rotary converters	455.2 p.355
Static multipliers induction heat	665.2 p.567
Static, phase converter	455.2 p.355
Stationary appliance, definition	550.2 p.481
Stationary motors 2 hp	430.109(C) p.331
Stationary motors frame grd.	430.242 p.335
Steady-state voltage	708.22(C) p.639
Steam, conductors in raceway	300.8 p.140
Steel cable tray, as equip. grd. cond.	T.392.60(A) p.244
Steel plate, protection	300.4(A1) p.136
Steel reinforcing bars	250.52(A31) p.112
Steel siding, bonding	250.116 I.N. p.122
Step and touch voltages	682.33 p.592
Stepdown auto-transformer	210.6(C2) p.50
Stepping masts	555.13(B1) p.514
Sticks, busway	368.12 p.225
Stiffen at temperatures	310.10 I.N. p.147
Stock rooms, aircraft hangars	513.1 p.422
Storable pool, definition	680.2 p.576
Storable pools, GFCI	680.32 p.585
Storage batteries	Art. 480 p.359
Storage batteries, solar	690.71 p.605
Storage battery, emerg. system	700.12(A) p.624
Storage battery, not over 250v	480.6 p.360
Storage battery, standby system	701.12(A) p.629
Stored energy operator	490.21(E5) p.362
Stored energy	692.56 p.609
Straight lines, underfloor raceway	390.9 p.239
Straight tubular lamps	410.130(E2) p.287
Straight voltage rating	240.85 p.97
Strain insulators open-conductors	225.12 p.72
Strain relief connector	314.23(H1) p.181
Strain relief mobile home cord	550.10(B) p.482
Strain relief on plug	555.19(A2) p.515
Stranded conduct. on fixt. chains	410.56(E) p.284
Stranded type, outdoor lampholders	225.24 p.73
Strap of switch	404.10(B) p.268
Stress reduction means	300.40 p.146
Strike termination devices	250.53(B) p.112
Strike termination devices	250.60 p.113
Strip heaters	427.2 I.N. p.307
Strong chlorides	330.12 p.193
Structural applications	110.11 I.N. #2 p.35
Structural ceiling, susp. ceiling	110.26(E1d) p.39
Structural steel, bonding	250.104(C) p.120
Strut-type channel raceway, cond. fill	T.384.22 p.236
Studios, feeders 400%	530.18(B) p.474
Studs, bushing for cable	300.4(B1) p.136
Subdivided load 48 amps	422.11(F) p.291
Subdivided load, heat 48 amps	424.22(B) p.297
Subject to strain or phys. damage	410.62(C) p.284
Submersible deep well pumps, Grd.	250.112(L) p.121
Submersible pump, fountain	680.51(B) p.588
Submersible pumps	501.140(A)(3) p.385
Submersion, occasional prolonged	T.110.28 p.41
Substantial linoleum	390.4(D) p.238

Entry	Reference
Substantially increased	300.21 p.144
Substation, Definition	225.2 p.71
Substation, fence height	110.31 p.40
Substations, warning signs	225.70 p.77
Suction systems	517.34(A1) p.448
Suddenly moving parts	240.41(B) p.96
Sufficiently low impedance	250.4(B4) p.103
Suffixes	310.120(C) p.173
Suitable balcony	430.232(2) p.335
Suitable covers on boxes	300.31 p.145
Suitable for wet locations	410.10(A) p.281
Suitable wiring methods	110.8 p.35
Suites, guest rooms	210.18 p. 52
Sulfur hexafluoride breaker	230.204(A) p.87
Sulfur hexafluoride circuit breaker	225.51 p.76
Sulfur hexafluoride gas	326.112 p.191
Summation of the currents	430.24 ex.3 p.318
Sump pumps	517.34(A2) p.448
Sunlight	378.12 (3) p.231
Sunlight effects	352.100 p.210
Sunlight resistance	553.7(B) p.512
Sunlight resistance	555.13(A2) p.514
Sunlight resistant jacket	350.2 p.207
Sunlight-resistant	336.12(3) p.199
Sunlight-resistant marking	400.6(B) p.260
Sunlight-resistant marking	402.9(B) p.266
Sunlight-resistant markings	352.120 p.211
Sunlight-resistant solar cable	690.31(C) p.601
Supervised industrial install., services	240.90 p.98
Supplemental electrode	250.53(D2) p.113
Supplemental, grounding electrode	250.53(2) p.112
Supplementary overcurrent devices	240.10 p.91
Support hardware	300.6(A) p.139
Support of cables with conduit	300.11(B) p.141
Support of ceiling fans	422.18 p.293
Support of fixtures, PVC conduit	352.12(B) p.209
Support of outlet box, #6 or larger	314.27 ex. p.182
Support wires, to be taut	314.23(D2) p.181
Supported independently of box	410.36(A) p.282
Supporting screws for yokes	250.146(B) p.127
Supports for ceiling fans	422.18 p.293
Supports for paddle fans	314.27(C) p.183
Supports for rigid conduit	T.344.30(B2) p.205
Supports for romex	334.30 p.197
Supports, vertical raceways	T. 300.19(A) p.143
Surface heating elem., subdivided	422.11(B) p.291
Surface heating elements 60 amp	422.11(B) p. 291
Surface marking of conductors	310.120(B1) p.173
Surface metal raceway, grounding	386.60 p.237
Surface metal raceways, voltage	386.12 p. 236
Surface mining machinery	90.2(B2) p. 22
Surface nonmetal. raceways, volts	388.12(3) p.237
Surface nonmetallic, dry location	388.10(1) p.237
Surface raceways	Art. 386 p.236
Surface raceways, splices & taps	386.56 p.237
Surface temperatures	547.4 p.478
Surface tracking	310.10(E) ex.1A p.148
Surface-mounted incandescent	410.16(C2) p.281
Surface-type snap switches	398.42 p.250
Surge arrester, 600v service	230.209 p.88
Surge arrester, grounding	280.25 p.133
Surge arrester, service	230.82(4) p.86
Surge arresters definition	DEF100 p.32
Surge-Protective Devices	Art. 285 p.133
Surrounding metal by induction	300.20(A) p.144
Suspended ceiling	314.23(D) p.180
Suspended ceiling panels	300.23 p.145
Suspended ceiling, struc. ceiling	110.26(E1d) p.39
Suspended ceilings	410.36(B) p.282
Suspended ceilings, enclosure size	314.23(D) p.180
SWD, switches as breakers	240.83(D) p.97
Swimming pool water heaters	680.9 p.577
Swimming pools	Art. 680 p.575
Swimming pools, radiant heaters	680.27(C3) p.585
Swimming pools,equip. submersion	680.23(A7) p.580
Switch loop, cable	200.7(C1) p.47
Switch loops	404.2(A) ex. p.266
Switch point less than 8", free cond.	300.14 p.142
Switch, air	230.204 p.87
Switch, bypass isolation	DEF 100 p.32
Switch, enclosure junction box	312.8 p.175
Switch, isolating	230.204(D) p.88
Switch, oil	230.204(A) p.87
Switch, oil	DEF 100 p.34
Switch, outlet, and tap devices	334.40(B) p.198
Switch, vacuum	230.204(A) p.87
Switch, wall	210.70(A1) ex. p.58
Switchboard, as service, bonding	408.3(C) p.274
Switchboard, bottom clearance	408.5 p. 275
Switchboard, dead front	520.21 p.461
Switchboard, live parts	T.110.26(A1) p.38
Switchboard, metal hood stage	520.24 p.461
Switchboard, pilot light	520.53(G) p.464
Switchboard, spacing to ceiling	408.18(A) p.275
Switchboards	Art. 408 p.274
Switchboards, dedicated space require.	110.26(E) p.39
Switched lampholder	410.93 p.285
Switches, ungrounded wire	404.2(A) p.266
Switches, 3-way & 4-way connect.	404.2 p.266
Switches, 600 volt knife	404.16 p.270
Switches, AC snap	404.14(A) p.269
Switches, AC-DC snap 50%	404.14(B2) p.269
Switches, bull	530.15(D) p.473
Switches, circuit breaker used as	404.11 p.268

Switches, CO/ALR snap 20 amp	404.14(C) p.269
Switches, double-throw knife	404.6(B) p.267
Switches, enclosure	404.3 p.267
Switches, faceplates thickness	404.9(C) p. 268
Switches, flashers	600.6(B) p.520
Switches, foot shield	665.7(B) p.567
Switches, fused not in parallel	404.17 p.270
Switches, garbage disposal	422.33 p.293
Switches, gas pumps double-pole	514.11(A) p.428
Switches, grounded conductor	404.2(B) ex. p.266
Switches, highest position	404.8(A) p.268
Switches, horsepower rated	430.109(A1) p.331
Switches, indicating off-on	404.7 p.267
Switches, inductive load	404.14(B2) p.269
Switches, isolat. Class I, Div.2	501.115(B2) p.383
Switches, isolating	404.13(A) p.269
Switches, manual adjustment	404.5 ex. p.267
Switches, motor control & disc.	430.111 p.332
Switches, mounting surface-type	404.10(A) p.268
Switches, mounting yoke	404.10(B) p.268
Switches, oil motor disconnect	430.111(B3) p.332
Switches, operating handle height	404.8(A) p.267
Switches, pendant-surface-knife	404.3 ex.1 p.267
Switches, plaster ears	404.10(B) p.268
Switches, plates	404.9 p.268
Switches, simultaneously disc.	404.2(B) ex. p.266
Switches, surface-type snap	398.42 p.250
Switches, thermostatically	424.20 p.297
Switches, time, flashers 6"	404.5 ex. p. 267
Switches, T-rated	404.14(B3) p.269
Switches, voltage between 300v	404.8(B) p. 268
Switches, wet location	404.4 p.267
Switches, wire bending space	404.18 p.270
Switches. marking	404.15(A) p.270
Switching device, lampholder	410.104(B) p.286
Switching the grounded conductor	514.11(A) p.428
Synch. motors of low torque	T.430.52 note 3 p.323
Synchronous generators	705.143 p.635

-T-

Table 1 Percent of fill conduit	p.711
Table 352.44 PVC thermal expansion	p.210
Table 5 insulated conductors area sq.in.	p.716
Table 5(A) aluminum conduct. sq. in. area	p.720
Table 8 DC resistance values	p.721
Table 9 AC resistance values	p.722
Table C1 conductors in conduit (fill)	p.745
Table C1 Fixture wire percent of fill	p.745
Table C1A compact conductors	p.749

Tamper resistant receptacles	517.18(C) p.444
Tanks	225.19(B) p.73
Tap conductors	240.4(E) p.90
Tap conductors, fixtures	410.117(C) p.286
Tap conductors, outdoors	240.21(B5) p.93
Taper per foot, conduit	500.8(E) p.375
Taper per foot, IMC conduit	342.28 p.202
Taper per foot, rigid conduit	344.28 p.204
Taps, cords not permitted	400.9 p.260
Taps, feeder not over 10'	240.21(B1) p.92
Taps, feeder not over 25'	240.21(B2) p.93
Taps, feeder over 25'	240.21(B4) p.93
Taps, flat cable	322.56(B) p.188
Taps, motor feeder	430.28 p.318
Taps, overcurrent protection	240.4(E) p.90
Task illumination	517.33(A) p.448
Task illumination, definition	517.2 p.442
Taut	314.23(D2) p.181
TC cable uses permitted	336.10 p.199
Technical equipment ground	647.6(B) p.563
Telephone cables, splicing	800.48 *I.N. #2* p.671
Telephone cond. pairs	T.400.4 note 7 p.257
Telephone wires below power	800.44(A1) p.671
Telescoping sections of raceway	250.98 p.118
Television equipment	Art. 810 p.682
Television studios	Art. 530 p.472
Temp. rating, ampacity of conductor	110.14(C) p.36
Temper.-actuated device	424.22(D3) p.298
Temperature in excess	350.12(2) p.207
Temperature in fixtures	410.115 p.286
Temperature limitations	110.14(C) p.36
Temperature ratings	110.14(C) *I.N.* p.36
Temperature rise, motors	430.32(A1) p.319
Temperature rise, reactors	470.18(E) p.359
Temperature zone, climatic	T.626.11(B) p.549
Temperature, ambient	310.15(3)(1) p. 149
Temperature, busways	368.238 p.226
Temperature, conductor limits	310.15 *I.N.* p.149
Temperature, hot to cold sealing	300.7(A) p.140
Temperature-limiting means	422.46 p.294
Temporary currents	250.6(C) p.103
Temporary lighting receptacles	590.4(D) p.517
Temporary lighting, tents, protection	525.21(B) p.471
Temporary power-light. permitted	590.3(C) p.517
Temporary submersion	T.110.28 p.41
Temporary wiring 90 days	590.3(B) p.516
Temporary wiring, emerg & tests	590.3(C) p.517
Temporary wiring, feeders originate	590.4(B) p.517
Temporary wiring, GFCI	590.6(A) p.518
Temporary wiring, guarding	590.7 p.518
Temporary wiring, lamp protection	590.4(F) p.517
Temporary wiring, removal immed.	590.3(D) p.517

Temporary wiring, romex	590.4(B & C) p.517	Thermal protector	410.130 (E2) p.287
Temporary wiring, splice	590.4(G) p.517	Thermal protector	DEF 100 p. 33
Temporary wiring, tests	590.6(B2a) p.518	Thermal resistivity	310.60(A) p.158
Tension take-up device	368.56(B2) ex. p.226	Thermal resistivity, Definition	310.2 p.147
Tension will not be transmitted	400.10 p.260	Thermal shock, diffusers	410.10(C2) p.281
Tension, fixture	410.56(F) p.284	Thermally noninsulating sand	424.41(E) p.299
Terminal fitting, raceway	300.5(H) p.139	Thermally protected, simple ballast	410.130(E2) p.287
Terminal housings, motors	430.12(A) p.314	Thermionic tubes Class I	501.105(A) p.382
Terminal or bus, grounded conductors	225.38(C) p.75	Thermopl. insul., deformed	310.10 *I.N.* p.147
Terminating seal MI cable	332.40(B) p.195	Thermopl. insul. may be deform.	402.3 *I.N.* p.262
Termination fittings, MI cable	501.10(B4) p.376	Thermopl. insul. may stiffen	402.3 *I.N.* p.262
Test, cords	590.6(B2a) p.518	Thermoplastic insul., stiffen	310.10 *I.N.* p.147
Test, emergency systems	700.3 p.622	Thermosetting insulation, organs	650.6(B) p.565
Test, equip. grounding cond.	590.6(B2) p.518	Thermostatically controlled	424.20 p.297
Test, ground fault on site	230.95(C) p.87	Thermostats	424.20 p.297
Test, heating cable	424.45 p.300	Thickness of metal boxes	314.40(B) p.184
Test, mobile home wiring	550.17 p.487	Thickness of sealing compound	501.15(C3) p.379
Test, receptacles	590.6(B2a) p.518	Thorium	500.6(B1) *I.N.* p.372
Test, recreational vehicle	551.60 p.500	Threaded hubs, bonding	250.92(B2) p.117
Test, service GFCI	230.95(C) p.87	Threaded couplings, bonding	250.92(B2) p.117
Test, standby systems	701.3(B) p.627	Threaded enclosure	314.23(E) p.181
Test, temporary wiring	590.3(C) p.517	Threaded hubs, box without device	314.23(E) p.181
Tests, pre-energization	225.56 p.76	Threaded wrenchtight	314.23(E) p.181
Theater, manual switches	700.21 p.626	Threaded, rigid conduit taper	344.28 p.204
Theaters	Art. 520 p.459	Threadless concrete couplings	342.42 p.203
Theaters, border lights	520.44 p.462	Threadless connectors, Rigid conduit	344.42(A) p.205
Theaters, cord connectors	520.67 p.467	Threads, 41/2 engaged	500.8(E1) ex. p.375
Theaters, curtain machines	520.48 p.463	Threads, five fully engaged	500.8(E1) p.375
Theaters, dimmers	520.25 p.461	Threads, taper per foot rigid steel	344.28 p.204
Theaters, festoon wiring	520.65 p.467	Threads, taper per foot, IMC conduit	342.28 p.202
Theaters, footlights	520.43 p.462	Threads, taper per foot, NPT die	500.8(E) p.375
Theaters, gutter or wireway fill	520.6 p.460	Three-way switches	404.2(A) p.266
Theaters, metal hood switchboard	520.24 p.461	Three-wire D.C. circuits	240.15(B4) p.92
Theaters, permitted wiring methods	520.5 p.460	Through-wall lighting assembly, pool	680.2 p.576
Theaters, portable power disb. box	520.62 p.466	Thunderstorm days	800.90(A) *I.N. #3* p.672
Theaters, proscenium lights	520.44 p.462	THW insulation, 90° C	T.310.104(A) p.169
Theaters, receptacles	520.45 p.463	THW insulation, ballast compart.	410.68 p. 285
Theaters, scenery	520.63 p.466	Tidal fluctuation	555.2(1) p.513
Theaters, special effects	520.66 p.467	Tidal fluctuation	682.2 DEF p.591
Theaters, switchboards metal hood	520.24 p.461	Tide level, marinas	555.2(1) p.513
Therapeutic pools	680.60 p.589	Tie ampacity, transformer	450.6(A2) p.351
Therapeutic pools, GFCI	680.62(A) p.589	Tie conductors, transformer	450.6(A4)(B) p.351
Therapeutic tub, lighting fixtures	680.62(F) p.590	Tie wires, knobs #8	398.30(E) p.250
Thermal barrier, resistors 12"	470.3 p.359	Tie wires, secure cables	300.19(C3) p.144
Thermal contraction, raceways	300.7(B) p.140	Time delay restarting load	455.22 *I.N.* p.357
Thermal cutouts number/location	T.430.37 p.321	Time delay, motor-comp.	440.54(B) p.346
Thermal devices for motors only	240.9 p.91	Time switches, flashers	404.5 p. 267
Thermal expansion	378.44 p.232	Toasters	422.4 p.290
Thermal expansion or contraction	352.44 p.210	Tool heads	T.430.22(E) p.317
Thermal expansion, raceways	300.7(B) p.140	Tools, portable grounded	250.114 p.121
Thermal protection required	410.130(E) p.287	Top shield, FCC cable	324.40(C1) p.190
Thermal protection, ballasts	410.130(E1) p.287	Torque motor, disconnecting means	430.110(B) p.332

Entry	Reference
Torque motors	430.7(C) p.312
Torque requirements for controls	430.9(C) p. 314
Torque tightening	110.14 I.N. p.36
Total hazard current	517.160(B) ex. p.458
Total hazard current, definition	517.2 p.442
Totally enclosed motors	501.125(A2) p.383
Towel bars	680.43(D) ex. p.587
Towers or poles, disconnect means	225.32 ex.3 p.74
Toxicity characteristics, ENT	362.100 p.222
Tracer in braid, cords	400.22(B) p.261
Track as circuit conductor	610.21(F4) p.530
Track conductors	410.155(A) p.289
Track lighting, voltages	410.155(A) p.289
Track load, fixtures	410.151B p.289
Trademark electrical equipment	110.21 p.37
Trailing cable	90.2(B2) p.22
Trailing cable and couplers	250.188(F) p.131
Tramrail track	610.21(F) p.530
Transf. over 600v, sec. O.C.P.	T.450.3(B) n.2 p.349
Transfer capability	310.60(A) p.158
Transfer equipment, emerg. systems	700.5 p.623
Transformer sec., without O.C.P.	240.21(C) p.93
Transformer vault, construction	450.42 I.N. #2 p.354
Transformer vault, fire protection	450.47 p.355
Transformer vault, natural circulation	450.45c p.355
Transformer, askarel-insulated	450.25 p.353
Transformer, case not grounded	250.21(A3) p.104
Transformer, doorways	450.43(A) p.354
Transformer, drainage	450.46 p.355
Transformer, dry-type	450.21(A) p.352
Transformer, dust	502.100(A1) p.388
Transformer, fire pump	695.5(B) p.618
Transformer, flammable liquids	450.23(A1) p.353
Transformer, grounded shield	426.31 p.306
Transformer, heat increase	450.3 I.N. #2 p.348
Transformer, individual	450.2 p.348
Transformer, isolation	427.26 p.309
Transformer, nameplate	450.11 p.352
Transformer, pool	680.23(A2) p.580
Transformer, readily accessible	450.13 p.352
Transformer, stepdown	210.6(C2) p.50
Transformer, zig-zag	450.5 p.350
Transformers	450.2 p.348
Transformers, askarel-ins.	450.25 p.353
Transformers, auto sprinklers	450.43(A) ex. p.354
Transformers, carbon dioxide	450.43(A) ex. p.354
Transformers, chimney-flue	450.25 p.353
Transformers, circuits derived from	215.11 p.60
Transformers, combustible material	450.22 p.353
Transformers, current	250.172 ex. p.129
Transformers, dampers	450.45(E) p.355
Transformers, dielectric fluid	450.24 p.353
Transformers, donut-type	450.5(A3) I.N. p.350
Transformers, door locks	450.43(C) p.354
Transformers, drainage	450.46 p.355
Transformers, electric furnace	450.26 ex.3 p.353
Transformers, fire resistant	450.21(B) ex. 1 p.352
Transformers, frequency	450.11 p.352
Transformers, gases	450.25 p.353
Transformers, halon	450.43(A) ex. p.354
Transformers, impedance	450.11 p.352
Transformers, instrument	250.178 p.129
Transformers, insulating liquid	450.11 p.352
Transformers, located 12"	450.22 p.353
Transformers, location	450.13 p.352
Transformers, marking	450.11 p.352
Transformers, nameplate	450.11 p.352
Transformers, outline lighting	600.21 p.522
Transformers, over 112 1/2 kva	450.21(B) p.352
Transformers, over 35,000v vault	450.21(C) p.353
Transformers, over 35kv in vault	450.24 p.353
Transformers, overcurrent prot.	450.6(B) p.351
Transformers, poorly vented	450.25 p.353
Transformers, potential	408.52 p.277
Transformers, pressure-relief vent	450.25 p.353
Transformers, readily accessible	450.13 p.352
Transformers, rooms fire resistant	450.21(B) p.352
Transformers, secondary ties O.C.P.	450.6(B) p.351
Transformers, sill height	450.43(B) p.354
Transformers, storage in vaults	450.48 p.355
Transformers, subtract.-connect.	450.5(A3) I.N. p.350
Transformers, supply points tie	450.6(A2) p.351
Transformers, T-connected	450.5 p.350
Transformers, temperature class	450.11 p.352
Transformers, tie ampacity	450.6(A2) p.351
Transformers, vault 35kv	450.24 p.353
Transformers, vault door	450.43 p.354
Transformers, vault door vent size	450.45(C) p.355
Transformers, vault read. accessible	450.13 p.352
Transformers, vent openings	450.45(A) p.355
Transformers, ventilation	450.9 p.352
Transformer-type rectifier	650.4 p.564
Transient motor	430.52(C3) I.N. p.323
Transient voltage surge supressors	285.1 p.133
Transient voltages	285.1 p.133
Transition assembly	324.2 p.189
Transitory overvoltages	450.5(C) p.350
Translucent material	516.4(C) p.436
Transmission of noise or vibration	400.7(A7) p.260
Transmission of noise, vibration	422.16(A) p. 292
Transmission of stresses	342.30(B2) p.203
Transmission of stresses	344.30(B2) p.205
Transmitting stations, ground. cond.	810.58(B) p.685
Transport refrigerated units	626.30 p.551

Transposing cable size	314.28(A2) p.183		
Transverse raceway, header	372.5 p.228		-U-
Transverse raceway, header	374.2 p.229		
Transversely routed, cablebus	370.6(B) p.227		
Travel plazas, truck	626.2 *I.N.* p.547	UF cable	Art. 340 p.201
Travel trailer definition	551.2 p.491	UF cable, 90°C	340.10(4) p.201
Traveling cables, lighting #14	620.12(A1) p.535	UF cable, 90°C	334.112 p.198
Traveling cables, signaling #20	620.12(A1) p.535	UF cable, ampacity	340.80 p.201
Traveling cables, supports	620.41 p.539	UF cable, burial depth	Table 300.5 p.138
Traveling carnival, discon. means	525.21(A) p.471	UF cable, uses permitted	340.10 p.201
Tray cable, uses permitted	336.10 p. 199	Ultimate insulation temp.	400.5(B) p.258
Trees, light fixtures outdoors	410.36(G) p.283	Ultimate insulation temperature	T.520.44 p.463
Trees, live vegetation	225.26 p.73	Unattended self-service stations	514.11(C) p.429
Trench, cond. derating factor	310.15(3A3) p.152	Unattended service station, discon.	514.11(C) p.429
Trench, conductors run together	300.5(I) p.139	Unattended service stations, emerg.	514.11(C) p.429
Trench-type flush raceway	390.4(C) p.238	Unbroken lengths, surface raceway	386.10(4) p.236
Trench-type raceways	390.4(C) p.238	Unbroken lengths, wireways	376.10(4) p.230
Trimming flex.metal conduit	348.28 p.206	Under raised floors, computer	645.5(E) p.561
Trimming, PVC conduit	352.28 p.209	Underfl. flat-top race., concrete cov.	390.4(D) p.238
Trip coils number & location	T.430.37 p.321	Underfloor raceways	Art. 390 p.238
Trip free breakers	240.80 p.97	Underfloor raceways, conductors	390.5 p.239
Trip setting	230.208 p.88	Underfloor raceways, disc. outlet	390.8 p.239
Trip-free circuit breakers	490.21(A2)(2) p.361	Underfloor raceways, loop wiring	390.7 p.239
Tripods, fixtures	410.36(C) p.283	Underground block distribution	800.47(B) p.671
Trolley frame, grounding	610.61 p.532	Underground cable under a bldg.	300.5(C) p.137
Trolley wires, ground return	110.19 p.37	Underground excavators	490.51(A) p.365
Troubleshooting	690.13 *I.N.* p.599	Underground feeder	Art. 340 p.201
TRU	626.2DEF p.548	Underground installations 600v	300.50 p.146
Truck panels	230.204 ex. p.87	Underground metal elbow	250.86 ex.3 p.117
Truck parking spaces	Art. 626 p.547	Underground pull box, over 600v	110.31(B1) p.40
Tube support, signs	600.41(B) p.524	Underground raceway, raceway seal	225.27 p.74
Tubes	230.52 p.83	Underground splice kit, services	230.46 p.82
Tubing, over 1000v marking	410.146 p.289	Underground tanks	250.52(A8) pg.112
Tubular heaters	427.2 *I.N.* p.307	Underground wiring gas station	514.8 p.428
Tungsten-filament lamp	404.14(A2) p.269	Underground, ducts	310.60(A) p.158
Tunnels, conductors & cables protect.	110.51(C) p.44	Underwater lights, pool	680.23 p.580
Tunnels, discharge lamps	210.6(D1b) p.50	Underwater speakers, pool	680.27(A1) p.585
Tunnels, high volt. power distribution	110.51(A) p.43	Unfinished accessory buildings	210.8(A2) p.50
Tunnels, high voltage conductors	110.53 p.44	Unfinished basements, GFCI	210.8(A5) p.50
Turbine, wind	Art. 694 p.610	Ungrounded conductor change in size	240.23 p.95
Turning vanes	424.59 *I.N.* p.300	Ungrounded control circuits	685.14 p.593
Turntables	T.430.22(E) p.317	Ungrounded control circuits	522.25 p.470
Twisted or cabled, pendant cond.	410.54(C) p.283	Ungrounded systems	250.32(C) p.109
Two locknuts, bonding	250.97 ex.2 p.118	Unguarded live parts over 600v	T.110.34(E) p.43
Two wire branch circuit, feeder	225.39(B) p.75	Unigrounded primary systems	280.24(B1) p.132
Two-fers, stage adapters	520.69 p.467	Uninterruptible power supplies	645.11 p.562
Two-wire DC systems	250.162(A) p.128	Uniquely polarized	604.6(C) p.526
Type IC, recessed fixture clearance	410.116(A2) p.286	Unit equipment	701.12(G) p.630
Type LFNC-A,	DEF. 356.2(1) p.216	Unit equipment, branch circuit	700.12(F) p.625
Type LFNC-B,	DEF. 356.2(2) p.216	Unit lighting load	220.3 p.61
Type LFNC-C,	DEF. 356.2(3) p.216	Unit switch, heaters	424.19(C) p.297
Types of enclosures	110.28 p.39	Unstepping masts	555.13(B1) p.514

Unswitched porcelain type	422.48(A) p.295	Ventilated, aircraft hangars	513.3(D) p.423
Unswitched type lampholders	410.12 p.281	Ventilating equipment interlocked	516.3(F) p.436
Untrained, persons	90.1(C) p.22	Ventilation, battery rooms	480.9(A) p.360
Unused openings, boxes	110.12(A) p.35	Ventilation, computer/data room	645.5(D4) p.561
Unused openings, cabinets	110.12(A) p.35	Ventilation, motors	430.14(A) p.315
Unused openings, equipment	110.12(A) p.35	Ventilation, spray room	516.10(C4d) p.440
Unwired portion, exist. dwelling	220.87 p.69	Ventilation, transformer	450.45(A) p.355
UPS equipment	645.11 p.562	Vertical clearance roof	225.19 ex.4 p.73
UPS systems	645.11 p.562	Vertical conductor support	T.300.19(A) p. 143
Upturned lugs	110.14(A) p.36	Vertical Flame test	645.5(D6) *I.N.* p.561
Uranium	500.6(B1) *I.N.* p.372	Vertical metal poles cond. sup.	410.30(B6) p.282
Urban water-pipe areas	280.24(A1) p.132	Vertical or horizontal distances	250.110(1) p.120
Usage characteristics	400.9 p.260	Vertical raceways, cond. support	T.300.19(A) p.143
USDA	626.11 *I.N.* p.548	Vertical risers, support	342.30(B3) p.203
USE cable	Art. 338 p.200	Vertical rod, antennas	810.16(B) p.683
Utility power failure	225.38(A) p.75	Vertical shafts, spread of fire	300.21 p.144
Utility-interactive inverter	705.60 p.634	Vertical tray flame test	725.179(C) *I.N.* p.649
		Vertically from top of bathtub rim	410.10(D) p.281
		Vessel, definition	427.2 p.308
-V-		Vessel, stamped	424.72(A) p.301
		Vibration, enduring	545.13 p.478
		Video or radio frequency	T.400.4 note 7 p.257
Va per outlet, 180va	220.14(I) p.63	Viewing tables, lampholders	530.41 p.475
Vacuum cleaner cord	T.400.4 p.256	Visible gap, capacitors	460.24(B1) p.358
Vacuum tubes	665.2 p.567	Volatile disinfecting agents	517.60(A2) p.453
Vandalism	701.12 p.629	Volatile flammable liquid	DEF 100 p.33
Vapor removal	300.22(A) p.144	Volatile flammable liquids	511.3 p.420
Vapor seals, busway	368.234(A) p.226	Voltage colors, heating cables	424.35 p. 298
Vapor source	516.3(B5) p.434	Voltage converters, vehicle	551.20(B) p.491
Vapor stop	516.3(B5) p.434	Voltage drop 1 %	647.4(D2) p.563
Vapors and residues	516.4(B) p.436	Voltage drop 2.5 %	647.4(D) p.563
Vapors of chlorine	330.12(2B) p.193	Voltage drop, ampacities	310.15 *I.N.* p.149
Vapors or liquids	501.20 p.381	Voltage drop, branch circuit	210.19 *I.N. #4* p.53
Vapors, exposed to	110.11 p.35	Voltage drop, compensate cma	250.122(B) p.124
Vaportight	410.10(C2) p.281	Voltage drop, feeders	215.2 ex. 1 p.59
Varnished cambric tapes	Table 400.4 note 5 p.257	Voltage drop, fire pump	695.7(A) p.620
Varying duty	Definition 100 p.28	Voltage drop, fire pump running 5%	695.7(B) p.620
Varying electromagnetic field	665.2 p.567	Voltage drop, phase converters	455.6 *I.N.* p.356
Vault door vent size	450.45(C) p.355	Voltage marking on cables	725.179(L) p.650
Vault door, transformer	450.43 p.354	Voltage rating motors	430.83 p.328
Vault, transformer 35kv	450.21(C) p.353	Voltage stresses, insulation	310.10(E) *I.N.* p.148
Vaults, film storage	530.51 p.475	Voltage stresses, shielding	400.32 p.261
Vaults, storage	450.48 p.355	Voltage transformers	450.3(C) p.348
Vegetation as support	230.10 p.79	Voltage, 120/240	D. examples p.804
Vehicle, door attached garage	210.70(A2) p.58	Voltage, contact with bodies	517.64(A1) p.455
Vehicle, electric charging	511.10(B) p.422	Voltage, definition	Art. 100 p.33
Vehicle, lanes lighting	511.7(B1b) p.421	Voltage, limitations	300.2(A) p.135
Vehicle, mounted generator	250.34(B) p.110	Voltage, line to neutral	240.60(A2) p.97
Vehicle, self-propelled	511.1 p.419	Voltage, nominal 120/240	D. examples p.804
Vehicle, washing areas	410.10(A) p.281	Voltage, steady-state	708.22(C) p.639
Vending machines, GFCI	422.51 p. 295	Voltages, circuit operates	110.4 p.35
Vented cell flame arrestor	480.9(A) p.360	Voltages, step and touch	680.33 p. 586

Voltages, transient	285.1 p.133	Welder outlets, over 50 amps	210.23(D) p.55
Volt-amps per square foot	T.220.12 p.63	Welders	630.1 p.552
Volts and amps, appliances	422.60(A) p.295	Welders, ampacity	630.11 p.552
Volts and watts, appliances	422.60(A) p.295	Welders, ampacity resistance	630.31 p.553
Votage drop 1.5%	647.4(D) p.563	Welders, cable	630.41 p.554
Vulcanized types	400.36 p.262	Welders, duty-cycle	630.31(A2) p.553
		Welders, overcurrent	630.12(A) p.552
		Welders, resistance	630.31 p.553
		Welders, resistance O.C.P.	630.32(A) p.554
-W-		Welders, welds per hour	630.31 I.N. #3 p.553
		Welding cable, dedicated cable tray	630.42(C) p.554
Wading pool, definition	680.2 p.576	Well casings	250.112(M) p.121
Wall space, room dividers	210.52(A2)(3) p.56	Wellways, escalators	620.4 p.533
Wall switch	210.70(A1) p.58	Wet bar sink	210.8(A7) p.50
Wall-mounted ovens,	T.220.55 demands p. 66	Wet location	DEF 100 p.30
Wall-mounted ovens, cord connect.	422.16(B3) p.292	Wet location, cut-out box	312.2 p.174
Wall-mounted ovens, grounding	250.140 ex. p.126	Wet locations	300.6(D) p.140
Wallpaper, heating cables	424.42 p.299	Wet locations, boxes	314.15 p.177
Walls frequently washed 1/4" space	300.6(D) p.140	Wet locations, fixtures	410.10(A) p.281
Walls, grounded	T.110.26(A) condition 2 p.38	Wet locations, lampholders	410.96 p.285
Warehouse demand factor	T.220.42 p.64	Wet locations, receptacles	406.9(B) p.272
Warning of derangement	700.6(A) p.623	Wet locations, switch/breaker	404.4 p.267
Warning ribbon, service laterals	300.5(D3) p.139	Wet locations, tools & appl.	250.114(D4) ex. p.122
Warning signs, Danger Hi-Voltage	490.55 p.365	Wet niche fixture, equip. grnd. cond.	680.25(B2) p.583
Warning signs, feeder	110.34(C) p.43	Wet-niche lighting fixture	680.23(B) p.580
Washer/dryer	Example D2b p.805	Wet-pit	501.140(A3) p.385
Washing machines, mobile home	550.16(B3) p.487	Wharves	555.1 p.513
Waste disposers, cord	422.16(B1) p.292	Wheelchair lift, duty rating	620.61(B4) p.542
Water Heater, cord-plug connected	422.16(A) p.292	Wheelchair lifts	620.1 p.532
Water heater, max. water temp.	422.47(1) p.294	Whip, fixture metal flex.	250.118(7B) p.123
Water heater, overcurrent protect.	422.11(E) p.291	White or letter W	200.10 (B1&2) p.48
Water heater, spa-hot tub	680.43(D5) p.587	White, conductor	200.7 p.47
Water heaters, branch circuit	422.13 p. 292	Wind turbine	Art. 694 p.610
Water hoses	668.31 p.571	Windblown dust	T.110.28 p.41
Water jets	680.43(D) ex. p.587	Winding with tape	400.10 I.N. p.260
Water level, pool maximum	680.2 DEF p.576	Windows, cords	400.11 p.260
Water meters	250.53(D1) p.113	Windows, service clearance	230.9(A) p.79
Water pipe ground	250.52(A) p.111	Wire bend. space, cab. wall opp.	T.312.6(B) p.176
Water pipes in vaults	450.47 p.355	Wire bending space, aluminum cond.	T.312.6(B) p.176
Water spray	450.43(A) ex. p.354	Wire bending space, cabinets	T.312.6(A) p.175
Water, navigable wiring under	555.13(B3) p.514	Wire bending space, motors	T.430.10(B) p.314
Waterfalls, stage lighting	520.66 p.467	Wire binding screws	110.14(A) p.36
Watt density, heating elements	426.20(A) p.305	Wire mesh, animal confine.	547.10(B) p.480
Wattage, marking	110.21 p.37	Wire pulling compounds	517.160(A6) p.457
Watt-hour meters	555.2 p.513	Wire, bus, screw	250.102(A) p.118
Wave action	555.2 p.513	Wired sections, heaters	424.12(B) p.296
Wave Shape, Nonlinear	DEF 100 p.28	Wiremold raceways	Art. 384 p.235
Weakening the building structure	300.4(A2) p.136	Wire-to-wire connections	T.430.12(B) p.315
Weatherproof faceplate, recept.	406.9(E) p. 273	Wireways, 30 conductors	376.22(B) p.230
Weep hole to discharge condensation	555.11 p.513	Wireways, dead ends	376.58 p.231
Weight, box support 50 pounds	314.27(A1) p.182	Wireways, extensions from	376.70 p.231
Weight, fixture 6 pounds	410.30(A) p.282	Wireways, extensions thru walls	376.10(4) p.230

Wireways, sound recording	640.7(A) p.556	X-ray, disconnect	660.5 p.566
Wireways, splices & taps 75%	376.56 p.230	X-ray, disconnect portable	517.72(C) p.455
Wireways, supports	376.30 p.230	X-ray, mobile definition	517.2 p.442
Wiring compartment	300.15(B) p.142	X-ray, mobile definition	660.2 p.565
Wiring in ducts, plenums	300.22(B) p.144	X-ray, momentary rating	660.2 p.565
Wiring methods, place of assembly	518.4 p.459	X-ray, nonmedical or nondental	660.1 p.565
Wiring on building surfaces	225.10 p.72	X-ray, portable definition	660.2 p.565
Wiring, factory-installed internal	90.7 p.24	X-ray, portable disconnect	517.72(C) p.455
Wiring, under navigable water	555.13(B3) p.514	X-ray, transportable	660.2 p.565
Withdrawal of conductors	300.17 p.142		
Within sight	DEF 100 p.29		
Within sight from	DEF 100 p.29		
Without permanent foundation	550.2 DEF p.481		
Witness test emergency system	700.3(A) p.622	-Y-	
Wood braces mounting boxes	314.23(B2) p.180		
Wood, fiber or plastic	424.42 p.299		
Wooden floors, open motors	430.14(B) p.316		
Wooden plugs	110.13(A) p.35	Yard and pier distribution systems	555.4 p.513
Wooden staves, pool bonding	680.42(B) p.586	Yellow color, heating cable 120v	424.35 p.298
Work areas	210.8(A2) p.50	Yellow conductor 3ø	517.160(A5) p.457
Work lights, plugging boxes	530.18(G) p.474	Yellow stripe, green conductor	250.119 p.123
Work space, access	110.33(B) p.42	Yellow stripes	250.119 p.123
Work surfaces counter tops	210.52(C) p.56	Yoke or strap, box	314.16(B4) p.178
Working clearance	110.26(A) p.38	Yoke, receptacle	DEF 100 p.31
Workmanlike manner	110.12 p.35	Yoke, multiple branch circuit	210.7 p.50
Workmanlike manner	800.24 p.670	Yoke, multiwire circuit	210.4(B) p.48
Workmanlike manner	820.24 p.687	Yokes	250.146(B) p.127
Workspace is illuminated	110.26(D) p.39		
Wound-rotor secondaries	430.32(E) p.320		
Wrenchtight threaded couplings	250.92(B2) p.117	-Z-	
Written record	230.95(C) p.87		
Written record	700.3(D) p.622		
Wye system, 6-phase	647.5 p.563	Z.P. marking	430.7 (14) p.312
		Zener diode barriers	504.50(A) *I.N.* p.396
		Zig-zag transformers	450.5 p.350
-X-		Zinc box thickness	314.40(B) p.184
		Zinc galvanized rods	250.52(A31) p.112
		Zinc	314.40(B) p.184
Xenon equipment	540.1 p.476	Zirconium	500.6(B1) *I.N.* p.372
Xenon projectors, cond. size	540.13 p.477	Zone 0 location, seals	505.16(A1) p.407
X-ray equip., capacity not over 60a	660.4(B) p.565	Zone directly over tub	410.10(D) p.281
X-ray equip., flexible cords	660.9 p.566	Zone for fire ladders	225.19(E) p.73
X-ray equip., noncurrent carrying parts	660.48 p.567		
X-ray equipment	Art. 660 p.565		
X-ray Equipment, ampacity	517.73(A1) p.455		
X-ray equipment, fixture wire	660.9 p.566		
X-ray equipment, individual B.C.	660.4(B) p.565		
X-ray equipment, O.C.P.	517.73(B) *I.N.* p.456		
X-ray feeders	660.6(B) p.566		
X-ray tubes, high voltage parts	660.47(A) p.566		
X-ray, attachment plug	517.72(C) p.455		
X-ray, conductors	660.6 p.566		

NOTES

NOTES

NOTES

NOTES

NOTES

Tom Henry's Code Electrical Classes Inc.

Since 1979 we have taught electrical exam preparation classes in 21 states, 84 cities and St. Croix in the Virgin Islands.

Schedule a class in your city by calling 1-800-642-2633.

Alabama
Birmingham, Huntsville, Mobile, Montgomery

Arkansas
Little Rock

Connecticut
Hartford

Florida
Fort Myers, Fort Lauderdale, Lakeland, Tampa, St. Petersburg, Bradenton, Sarasota, Winter Haven, Jacksonville, Ocala, Leesburg, Daytona Beach, Orlando, Kissimmee, Winter Park, Haines City, Cocoa Beach, Ft. Pierce, Naples

Georgia
Atlanta, Macon, Gainesville

Hawaii
Honolulu

Indiana
Fort Wayne, Indianapolis, South Bend, Evansville, Muncie, Kokomo, Michigan City, Elkhart

Iowa
Des Moines, Cedar Rapids

Kansas
Wichita, Manhattan, Topeka, Salina, Dodge City

Kentucky
Louisville, Owensboro, Lexington

Louisiana
New Orleans, Shreveport, Baton Rouge, Covington

Michigan
Detroit, Grand Rapids

Mississippi
Jackson

Missouri
St. Louis, Kansas City, Springfield, Joplin, St. Joseph

North Carolina
Raleigh

Ohio
Columbus, Cincinnati, Akron

Oklahoma
Oklahoma City

Pennsylvania
Allentown

South Carolina
Columbia, Greenville, Spartanburg

Tennessee
Chattanooga, Memphis, Knoxville, Johnson City, Nashville, Jackson

Texas
Dallas, Lubbock, Amarillo, Wichita Falls, Waco, Odessa, Corpus Christi, Abilene, Longview, Plainview, San Angelo, Houston, San Antonio, College Station

http://www.code-electrical.com

ENRY PUBLICATIONS SINCE 1985

ISBN 978-0-9801787-3-9